Instructor's Manual with Test Items
for

Counseling in Schools
ESSENTIAL SERVICES AND
COMPREHENSIVE PROGRAMS

Third Edition

John J. Schmidt
East Carolina University

D1115856

Allyn and Bacon
Boston • London • Toronto • Sydney • Tokyo • Singapore

ISBN 0-205-29283-6

Printed in the United States of America

10 9 8 7 6 5 4 3 2 1   01 00 99 98

Contents

Introduction   *1*

Chapter 1:   The School Counseling Profession   *3*

Counseling as a Profession
Development of School Counseling
Emergence of Guidance and Counseling in Schools
Expansion of School Counseling
A Professional Identity
Exercises and Test Questions

**Chapter 2:   Comprehensive School Counseling
                       Programs**   *11*

A Definition of School Counseling
The Purpose of School Counseling Programs
*Educational Development, Career Development, Personal
and Social Development*
A Comprehensive Program
Facilities and Resources
*The Counseling Center, Materials and Equipment, Budget,
Personnel*
Exercises and Test Questions

Chapter 3:   The School Counselor   *21*

Varying Roles of School Counselors
*The Elementary School Counselor, The Middle School
Counselor, The High School Counselor*
Training of School Counselors
*The Helping Relationship, Human Development, Group
Processes, Student Appraisal, Career Development Theory
and Information, Educational Research, Social and Cultural
Foundations, Ethical and Legal Issues, The School Setting*
Credentials of School Counselors
State Certification, National Certification
Exercises and Test Questions

Chapter 4:   Essential Services   *35*

Counseling
   *Individual Counseling, Group Counseling, Student
   Counseling, Parent and Teacher Counseling*
Consulting
   *Information Services, Instructional Services, Problem-
   Solving Services, Other School Services*
Coordinating
   *Data Collection and Sharing, Referrals and Follow-up,
   School-Wide Events*
Appraising
   Student Evaluation, Environmental Evaluation
Exercises and Test Questions

Chapter 5:   Developing a Comprehensive Program   *49*

Planning
   *Assessing the Current Program, Seeking Input and Support for
   change, Assessing Students', Parents' and Teachers' Needs,
   Determining Resources*
Organizing
   *Setting goals, Assigning Responsibilities, Marketing the
   Program*
Implementing
   *Scheduling Services and Setting Priorities, Balancing Time,
   Counseling, Consulting, Coordinating, Appraising*
Evaluating
Exercises and Test Questions

Chapter 6:   Individual Counseling and Group Procedures   *63*

What is Counseling?
Who Needs Counseling?
Goals of Counseling
Individual Counseling in Schools
   *Establishing a Relationship, Exploring Concerns, Taking
   Action, Ending the Relationship*
Brief Counseling
Crisis Counseling
Counseling Skills
Counseling Approaches and Models
   *Adlerian Counseling, Reality Therapy, Cognitive-
   Behavioral Counseling, Invitational Counseling*
Group Procedures
   A Rationale for Group Process, Group Counseling and Group

Guidance, Purpose and Nature of Groups, Leading Groups
Advantages of Group Counseling, Limitations of Group
Counseling, Advantages of Group Guidance, Limitations
of Group Guidance
Research on Counseling
Research on Groups
Group Guidance Research, Group Counseling Research
Exercises and Test Questions

Chapter 7:   **Collaboration with School and Agency**
                          Professionals   *77*

School Services
Parents and Guardians, Teachers, Principals, Nurses,
Psychologists, and Social Workers
Community Agencies
Health Departments, Mental Health Centers, Social
Services, Family Services, Private Practitioners
Counselors as Consultants
Consulting Processes, Consulting Skills
Research on Consulting
Exercises and Test Questions

Chapter 8:   **Student Appraisal**   *87*

Standardized Testing
Standardization, Selection of Tests, Validity and
Reliability, Usefulness
Using Standardized Tests
Test Security, Administration, Interpretation
Types of Assessment Instruments
Achievement Tests , Aptitude Tests, Interest Inventories,
Personality Inventories and Tests
Other Assessment Techniques
Observations, Interviews, Sociometric Methods, Child Study
Conferences, Biographical and Self-Expression Techniques
Exercises and Test Questions

Chapter 9:   **Educational Planning and Career**
                          Development   *99*

Primary Purpose of School Counseling
Educational Planning for All Students
Student Advocacy, Lifelong Learning
Career Planning and Decision-Making
Student Awareness, Exploration, Decision Making
Case Study of Johnny

Case Study of Gertrude
Exercises and Test Questions

**Chapter 10:   Evaluation of a School Counseling
                    Program   *107***

Types of Program Evaluation
  *Goal Attainment, Student Outcomes, Consumer
  Satisfaction, Expert Assessment*
School Counselor Evaluation
  *What Will Be Evaluated?, How Will Evaluation be Done?,
  Who Will Evaluate?, Performance Appraisal Processes and
  Instruments*
Exercises and Test Questions

Chapter 11:   Professional Ethics and Legal Issues   *117*

Ethical Standards for School Counselors
  *Responsibilities to Students, Responsibilities to Parents,
  Responsibilities to Colleagues and Professional
  Associates, Responsibilities to the School and
  Community, Responsibilities to Self, Responsibilities to
  the Profession, Maintenance of Standards*
The Nature of Law
  The Law and Schools, The Courts, School Board Policies
Legal Issues for School Counselors
  *Students' Rights, Parents' Rights, The Buckley Amendment,
  Public Law 94-142 329, Child Abuse, Counselor Liability,
  Title IX*
Exercises and Test Questions

Chapter 12:   School Counseling Today and Tomorrow   *129*

Students of Tomorrow
  *Remedial Concerns, Preventive Issues, Developmental
  Needs, Poverty, Diversity*
Schools of Tomorrow
  *Technology, Parental Involvement, Teacher Collaboration,
  School-Based Services, Youth Services*
The Future of School Counseling
Exercises and Test Questions

Introduction

This instructor's manual is a quick-reference companion for the text, *Counseling in Schools: Essential Services and Comprehensive Programs*, 3rd Edition. The manual provides a brief summary of each chapter and a synopsis that highlights significant content. Learning objectives are stated at the beginning of each chapter summary. In addition, each chapter of the text ends with exercises for students, and this manual offers a rationale for these activities. Sample test questions conclude each chapter in the manual.

Counseling in Schools traces the development of school counseling, presents contemporary roles and functions of today's school counselors, and explores future possibilities for the profession. This text is intended primarily for graduate courses that prepare students for a career in school counseling. As defined in this text, *school counseling* includes services designed to meet the needs of students, parents, and teachers during the elementary, middle, and high school years.

My experience in the school counseling profession includes nine years as a counselor in elementary, middle, and high school practice, five years as a school system director of counseling services, five years as the North Carolina coordinator of school counseling services with the Department of Public Instruction, and the remaining years as a professor of counselor education. With each passing year, I have become increasingly concerned about the profession and the ever-expanding job that school counselors face. Most notably, I am troubled by the inability of school counselors to provide direct services to students, parents and teachers in helping them reach educational and career goals. Similarly, I am bothered by people, professionals and lay-people alike, who minimize the important role that counselors have in schools and the contribution they can make to the overall educational program. Sometimes these people are counselors, themselves, who have a limited vision of what they can do to help students, parents and teachers. This restricted vision is tragic for counselors, their schools, communities, and the profession.

Despite these challenging observations, I am optimistic about the profession. This optimism is due largely to the energetic and enthusiastic students I see entering counselor education programs. For me, it has been a pleasure to teach them. My hope is that this text will serve to prepare future counselors who will maintain an enthusiastic and optimistic posture about who they are and what they offer to schools.

School counseling is one of several specialties that comprise the counseling profession. I believe school counselors are on equal footing with counselors who choose to practice in other specialty areas. Therefore, it is imperative that counselor education programs maintain high standards and offer an expanded curriculum for students entering the school counseling profession. I believe this book complements such an exemplary program.

In this third edition, I have added a chapter about how to develop a comprehensive school counseling program. This chapter might be viewed as the "practical" application of concepts related to program development and service delivery. It explores factors such as assessing needs, setting goals, balancing time, scheduling services, and other aspects of being a professional school counselor.

The exercises added to the second edition have been retained and in some cases expanded. These activities help students use the material in the chapters to internalize important concepts. They will help make the material come alive for your students. In this manual, I have included a rationale for each exercise to help you determine whether or not it fits your class presentation.

At the end of each chapter in the manual, I offer examination questions. Some of these are questions I have used in a course titled, "Development and Coordination of School Counseling Programs," and they are based on the content of the text.

The components of a comprehensive school counseling program, as advocated in this book, are the ideal elements and practices embraced by professional school counselors. Traditional roles and functions of school counselors have not always served the interests of students, parents, and teachers, nor have they helped to clarify the professional identity of school counselors. More important, traditional functions may no longer be relevant to meet the needs of future populations. In this text, I encourage students to embrace a futuristic and positive vision of what the school counseling profession should be today, and what it could become tomorrow. I hope you and your students realize that goal.

Jack Schmidt, Ed.D., LPC, NCC
Professor and Department Chair
Counselor and Adult Education Department
East Carolina University
Greenville, NC

Chapter 1

The School Counseling Profession

OBJECTIVES

1) Understand the relationship between school counseling and the broader counseling profession.

2) Learn about significant historical events and legislative actions that influenced the development of the school counseling profession.

3) Examine elements and issues related the professional identity of school counselors.

CHAPTER SUMMARY

School counselors are members of an extended helping profession that spans an array of services and includes practice in a variety of settings. In the United States, professional counselors work in hospitals, mental-health centers, industries, family centers, schools and other settings.

When compared with other notable vocations such as medicine, law, and teaching, school counseling is a relatively young profession, but its growth has been remarkable during the twentieth century, particularly in the United States. This chapter surveys the history of the counseling profession and the emergence of school counseling within that profession. In addition, this chapter discusses the importance of a professional identity for school counselors and the national associations that enhance this identity.

KEY CONCEPTS, EVENTS, NAMES, AND TERMS

Concepts and Events

- Ancient Greeks and democratic principles
- The middle ages and vocations
- Mental health movement and child guidance clinics
- Industrial Revolution
- Vocational guidance
- World War I and intelligence testing
- Development of counseling theory
- World War II and government influence
- George Barden Act of 1946
- *Guidance in the Curriculum* (ASCD, 1955)

<u>Concepts and Events</u> (con'd)
- Sputnik I and a national alarm
- National Defense Education Act of 1958 (NDEA)
- Family Educational Rights and Privacy Act of 1974
- Education Act for All Handicapped Children of 1975 (Public Law 94-142)
- *A Nation at Risk* report of 1983
- Identity for school counselors

<u>Names</u>

- Tomasco Garzoni
- Clifford Beers
- William Healy
- George Merrill
- Jesse B. Davis
- Eli Weaver
- Frank Goodwin
- Frank Parsons
- John Dewey
- C. Gilbert Wrenn
- E. G. Williamson
- Carl Rogers
- National Vocational Guidance Association
- American Personnel Guidance Association
- American Association for Counseling and Development
- American Counseling Association
- American School Counselor Association
- National Board of Certified Counselors (NBCC)
- Council for Accreditation of Counseling and Related Educational Programs (CACREP)

<u>Terms</u>

- Vocational guidance
- Trait and Factor Theory
- Client-centered therapy

CHAPTER SYNOPSIS

Counseling as a Profession

This section gives a historical perspective of professional helping beginning with ancient times and moving through the middle ages with early signs of vocational guidance. The 1890's and early 1900's frame the beginning of the school counseling profession.

Development of School Counseling

The school counseling profession began as a guidance movement that emerged from the Industrial Revolution at the beginning of the twentieth century. Early developments in the guidance movement were complemented by the creation of the National Vocational Guidance Association in 1913 (NVGA).

Emergence of Guidance and Counseling In Schools

The work of Jesse Davis, Anna Reed, Eli Weaver, Frank Parsons, and a host of other pioneers created the momentum for the development of a school counseling profession. Eventually, some leaders began encouraging a broader focus to include issues of human development beyond vocational guidance.

Before World War II
During the first World War, the U.S. military began using group-training procedures to screen and classify draftees. Intelligence testing, developed in the beginning of the decade, was the catalyst for this movement.

The 1920s also saw the rise of progressive education in the schools. This movement, introduced by John Dewey, emphasized the school's role in guiding students in their personal, social and moral development.

The late 1930s saw the first theory of guidance and counseling, called Trait and Factor Theory, developed by E. G. Williamson at the University of Minnesota. About the same time that Williamson and his colleagues were developing their directive counseling approach, others continued to question the narrow focus of the vocational guidance movement.

World War II to the Space Age
The 1940s saw major changes in the counseling profession and these developments had significant impact on the practice of counseling in schools. In addition, organizational changes within the profession and emerging theoretical models of counseling were significant influences during this period.

The Rogerian influence. Carl Rogers probably had more influence on the counseling profession and the development of counseling approaches than any single person.

World War II and government influence. Two other events that influenced the counseling profession during this period of time were World War II and increased government involvement in the counseling and psychology professions.
• *The George-Barden Act of 1946.*

- *Reorganization of the Guidance and Personnel Branch of the U.S. Office of Education.*
- *Soviet Sputnik I. and the National Defense Education Act*

Organizational changes and professional influences. As a result of these national initiatives and major events, the 1950s saw a continued acceleration of the school counseling profession. This included the establishment of the American Personnel and Guidance Association (APGA) in 1952.

Post 1960s

The 1960s saw continued development and expansion of the counseling profession. This was, in part, a result of legislation to increase services and enhance existing programs, and refinement and clarification of the role of the school counselor.

In addition, automation in industry would affect employment and career counseling for adults as well as for students in schools. Changing roles of women would affect family structures and the accelerated pace of society would increase daily stress in most people's lives. A number of other developments contributed to human challenges and critical decisions for which counselors were needed.

Federal legislation during this period continued to have an impact on the counseling profession and the role of counselors, particularly school counselors.
- *The Elementary and Secondary Education Act of 1965*

The 1960s saw a new, expanded role for school counselors with movement away from an emphasis on guidance programs.
- *The School Counselor* journal

Expansion of School Counseling

During the initial five decades of school counseling's development and growth, little was written or designed to help elementary counselors define and describe their role in schools.

In 1964, the government expanded NDEA to include elementary school counseling.

One event that helped elementary counselors identify their distinct role in the schools was a 1966 report by the Joint Committee on the Elementary School Counselor (ACES-ASCA, 1966).

Several studies encouraged the expansion of elementary

counseling. The proliferation of these studies gave visibility to elementary school counseling.

Elementary School Guidance and Counseling journal by the American School Counselor Association in the late 1960s.

A Nation At Risk report of 1983 focused on the declining achievement of U.S. students. "Effective schools" became synonymous with a call for accountability in the classroom and in special services such as school counseling programs.

During the 1980s, the need for school counselors to develop a clear identity and describe their role and functions at the various levels of school practice became paramount. Today as we rapidly approach the twenty-first century, this need to establish a clear professional identity continues.

A Professional Identity

In recent years, many authors have stressed the importance of counselors creating a clear identity and purpose for their role in schools. Despite this encouragement uncertainty about the school counselor's role continues.

School counselors historically have been thought of as different from counselors in clinical settings such as mental-health and family counseling centers. Inconsistent perceptions by administrators and teachers add to the confusion about the school counselor's role.

School counseling, as with many aspects of life, is cyclical in its development. As such, some events and ideas that contributed to its early development are seen again in current professional literature.

The future of school counseling as a profession depends on the ability of counselors to become an integral part of the school setting while maintaining their unique role and contribution to student welfare and development.

Exercises

1. In this introductory chapter you learned that the school counseling profession began as a reaction to social and political forces in the early 1900s. Over the next several decades the profession grew and changed as a response to other significant events in the United States and around the world. What relationship, if any, do you see with this heritage and the role of counselors in the school? Discuss this in a small group and ask someone to record the highlights of

your discussion to share with the class.

Rationale: One rationale for using this activity is that it helps students explore the school counseling profession as a "reaction" to national and world events. The question that remains is whether or not the profession will become "proactive" in seeking its place among the helping professions.

2. This chapter presented major events that contributed to the development of school counseling across this country. On your own or with a small group, research the development of school counseling in your state. What were major events, legislative action, or other occurrences that influenced the profession? *Rationale: This exercise will help students identify important regional and state events that have affected the school counseling profession. It may also heighten student awareness to the importance of being involved with professional organizations to stay informed of legislative and other important action.*

3. Professional identity is an important issue presented in this chapter. If you were hired by a school tomorrow as its new counselor, what five actions would you take to begin establishing a professional identity? Discuss and compare your actions with a group of your classmates. *Rationale: This exercise may help individual students become more intentional about their own professional identities.*

Test Questions

Multiple Choice Items

_(c)_ 1. The school counseling profession has its origin in the
(a) psychoanalytic movement of the early twentieth century.
(b) testing of soldiers during World War I.
(c) vocational guidance movement in the early 1900s.
(d) philosophy of the ancient Greeks.

_(a)_ 2. Clifford Beers was instrumental in the mental health movement as
(a) a hospitalized patient who wrote the book *A Mind That Found Itself.*
(b) founder of the Illinois Institute of Juvenile Research.
(c) developer of client-centered therapy.
(d) first president of the American Mental Health Association.

__(b)__   3. Jesse B. Davis, Frank Goodwin, Anna Reed, Eli Weaver, and Frank Parsons were
(a) early theorists in the counseling profession.
(b) some leaders of the early guidance movement.
(c) philanthropists who established grants for school counseling development.
(d) the first four presidents of the National Vocational Guidance Association.

__(b)__   4. The establishment of the National Vocational Guidance Association was the beginning of
(a) the merger of educational and psychological professions.
(b) the unification of the counseling profession of today.
(c) the American Psychological Association (APA).
(d) vocational education in this country.

__(a)__   5. A major historical event that created an atmosphere for propelling the school counseling profession was the
(a) launching of the Soviet Sputnik I in 1957.
(b) invention of television.
(c) invention of the personal computer.
(d) development of the *Army Alpha Examination* during World War I.

__(d)__   6. The federal bill that provided funds to train counselors for secondary schools during the late 1950s and early 1960s was
(a) the George-Barden Act.
(b) the Elementary and Secondary Education Act (ESEA).
(c) the Mental Health Act for Secondary Schools.
(d) the National Defense Education Act (NDEA).

__(b)__   7. The national journal that has complemented the growth of elementary school counseling is
(a) *Guidance in the Elementary Schools.*
(b) *Elementary School Guidance and Counseling.*
(c) *Journal of School Guidance.*
(d) *Child Development and Learning.*

__(a)__   8. Today the American School Counselor Association is a division of this national organization:
(a) the American Counseling Association (ACA)
(b) the American Psychological Association (APA)
(c) the National Guidance and Counseling Association (NGCA)
(d) the Association for Counseling Psychology (ACP)

_(c)_ 9. The newest accrediting body for counselor education in this country is
   (a) the National Council for Accrediting Teacher Education (NCATE).
   (b) the American Association for Counseling and Development (AACD).
   (c) the Council for Accreditation of Counseling and Related Educational Programs (CACREP).
   (d) the National Board of Certified Counselors (NBCC).

_(c)_ 10. One factor contributing to the school counseling profession's difficulty in establishing a clear identity is the
   (a) failure of school counselors to be as well-trained as other counselors.
   (b) inability of the national association to bring counselors together.
   (c) inconsistent use of terms to identify who school counselors are and what they do.
   (d) psychological profession's clear identity.

Matching Items

COLUMN A		COLUMN B
_(e)_	Frank Parsons	A. Trait Factor Theory
_(f)_	NDEA	B. Client-centered Therapy
_(a)_	E. G. Williamson	C. Wrote book about mental health institutions
_(d)_	Tomasco Garzoni	
_(b)_	Carl Rogers	
_(c)_	Clifford Beers	D. Published early book about occupations
_(g)_	Jesse B. Davis	
_(j)_	Public Law 94-142	E. Started Vocational Bureau in Boston
_(i)_	ACA	
_(h)_	Arthur Otis	F. Federal act in response to Soviet Sputnik I
		G. Began guidance classes in Michigan schools
		H. Developed group intelligence tests
		I. Association for professional counselors
		J. Federal act for educating exceptional students

Chapter 2

Comprehensive School Counseling Programs

OBJECTIVES

(1) Define and describe a comprehensive school counseling program and illustrate how its goals blend with the overall mission of the school.
(2) Describe the processes for establishing a school counseling program.
(3) Introduce the essential services in a school counseling program.
(4) Describe the necessary facilities, resources, and personnel of a comprehensive program.

CHAPTER SUMMARY

A school counseling program is a planned component of the larger school purpose and mission. The role of the school counselor is to design a comprehensive program of services with specific goals and objectives that complement the broader mission of the school.

This chapter presents the elements of a comprehensive school counseling program. It defines school counseling, states the purpose of school counseling programs, outlines the elements and services of a program, and surveys the facilities, materials, and personnel needed in a comprehensive program.

KEY CONCEPTS, EVENTS, NAMES, AND TERMS

Concepts and Events

- Consistent language
- Comprehensive school counseling program
- Educational development
- Career development
- Personal and social development
- Needs assessment
- Program evaluation
- Essential services
- Self-assessment

Names

- *The School Counselor*
- *Elementary School Guidance and Counseling*
- *Professional School Counseling*
- Alfred Adler

11

- School counseling
- Personnel services
- Developmental
  guidance and counseling
- Student Services Team
- Teacher-Advisee Program
- Parent Education Program
- Program phases: planning,
  organizing, implementing,
  and evaluating

- Guidance
- Counseling
- Consultation
- School-wide guidance
- Counseling Center
- Peer Helper Program
- Advisory Committee
- Appraising
- Counselor accountability
- Paraprofessionals

CHAPTER SYNOPSIS

A Definition of School Counseling

To be consistent in developing program descriptions, counselors will benefit from a language that is clear and understandable.

The following descriptions briefly define some of the major terms used in this text. In later chapters, these terms will be defined and described in greater detail.

Guidance
Counseling
Developmental Guidance
and Counseling
Consultation
Parent Education Program

Student Services Team
Counseling Center
Teacher-Advisee Program
Peer Helper Program
School-wide Guidance
Advisory Committee

The Purpose of School Counseling Programs

To some extent the struggle of the school counseling profession to develop a clear identity has contributed to the confusion about the purpose of employing counselors in school settings.

It is imperative that school counselors view their role, not as a series of unrelated crisis-oriented services, but rather as an orchestrated program of essential services and activities that complement the instructional program of the school. A key element in describing a comprehensive counseling program is the notion that these services are essential to the school.

Educational Development

The challenge in U.S. society today and in the future is to realize the belief that all children can learn, and to do so schools must create climates that give every student an equal opportunity to succeed academically. Counselors contribute to this goal by assessing students' abilities, guiding teachers in placing students in the instructional program, providing services for parents to learn about their children's development and progress in school, and counseling students about their goals and plans in life.

Career Development

The school counseling profession has its roots in vocational guidance, which remains a vital part of comprehensive school counseling programs.

As a lifelong process, career development is an important component of all school counseling programs, elementary through secondary schools.

Personal and Social Development

A third purpose of comprehensive school counseling programs is to facilitate the personal and social development of all students.

Comprehensive school counseling programs, by definition, are sensitive to multicultural perspectives and plan individual, group, and school-wide services accordingly.

What distinguishes the practice of school counselors at the three different levels are the developmental stages and needs indicated by the students in these schools. Nevertheless, there are some common processes and services used by school counselors across all the educational levels.

A Comprehensive Program

A comprehensive school counseling program consists of counseling, consulting, coordinating, and appraisal services offered in response to the identified needs, goals, and objectives of the school and community. A program occurs as a series of processes that include planning, organizing, implementing, and evaluating procedures.

Adequate and accurate program evaluation enables counselors to return to the initial goals and objectives of the program and assess what changes, if any, are needed. Figure 2-1 in the text illustrates this cycle of planning, organizing, implementing, and evaluating a counseling program.

Planning consists of procedures and decisions that help counselors evaluate school-wide goals; assess students', parents', and teachers' needs; and select goals and objectives for their counseling programs.

Organizing is a continuation of the planning process and includes the selection of major goals and objectives and a determination of which services can best address and meet these goals. Program organization also entails assignments and timelines for carrying out specific activities.

Implementing is the action phase of a comprehensive program. In this phase, all the services that constitute the program are delivered.

Evaluating consists of procedures that enable counselors to determine the success of their services, identify apparent weaknesses, and recommend program changes for the future.

In a comprehensive school counseling program, all the procedures associated with this cycle of planning, organizing, implementing, and evaluating are coordinated by the counselor in cooperation with the school principal, the advisory committee, and the supervisor of counseling services.

Facilities and Resources

School counselors have needs of their own and one need to have space in a counseling center.

The Counseling Center

Counseling centers in elementary schools, middle schools, and high schools vary due to the development needs of students, the size of the schools, and the types of major activities in those schools.

Design

Ideally, an elementary school counseling center includes a private office for sessions with students, parents, teachers, and others, with an adjoining, larger room for group sessions, play activities, and other services. In middle schools, counseling centers consist of one or more counselor's offices and a larger outer space for students to use books, computers, games, and other materials for self-instruction. Senior high counseling centers are similar to middle school designs except that in large high schools there are more offices for counselors, and space may be designated for career materials and equipment.

Location
Equally important to the design of a school counseling center is its location. The location should enhance its visibility, facilitate communication between all groups in the school, and invite people to enter and use its facilities.

Materials and Equipment
A well-designed counseling center is complete when it includes appropriate and adequate materials and equipment to deliver the intended services. A school counseling center is furnished with appropriate-size tables and chairs, and equipment to use with filmstrips, videos, computer programs, and other media. All counselors should have a telephone with a private line for consultations and referrals.

Budget

Materials and equipment need to be assessed annually as do other aspects of the counseling program. As items become worn or out-dated, they are replaced. Table 2-1 in the text illustrates items found in a budget for a school counseling program.

Personnel

Facilities, materials, equipment, and finances provide the physical structure and set fiscal limits for a school counseling program, but it is the people in the program who determine its true value and potential.

Counselors
The number of counselors hired in a school counseling program makes a difference in the quantity and quality of services offered. Usually schools employ enough counselors to meet the counselor to student ratios recommended by professional associations and accrediting organizations.

Clerical Assistants
Schools need sufficient clerical staff to help counselors and teachers perform their respective duties in a timely fashion. Excellent secretaries and technical assistants are indispensable in today's schools, and this is true for school counseling centers as well.

Paraprofessionals and Volunteers
Paraprofessionals are persons who have some training in human services and can assist counselors with academic advising, career

information, and other initial relationships. They can also perform clerical tasks as the need arises, as can volunteers in the school.

Volunteers offer valuable time to assist with many school services including those of a counseling program. Parents, grandparents, guardians, retired citizens, and other people comprise a large pool of available volunteers.

Exercises

1. Identify a school counselor in your community and make an appointment to visit and discuss the school counseling profession. During your visit, ask the counselor, "How do you plan services?" Ask the counselor if a written plan exists about the program. In class, share your observations about this counseling program. [NOTE: In sharing information about this interview, you should keep the counselor's name and the school's name confidential.]
   Rationale: Students learn best from discovering what is happening in the field of school counseling. I have found that these types of interviews help students observe what counselors are actually doing in terms of planning comprehensive programs. It allows them to see "good, bad and the ugly" of school counseling.

2. Remember when you were in elementary, middle, or high school? Do you remember a counseling center? What do you recall about this place? Share your recollections in a small group and compare similarities and differences.
   Rationale: By remembering their experiences as a student with former school counselors, students become sensitive to how others will view them in their future roles.

3. In a small group, take the four stages of a comprehensive program— planning, organizing, implementing, and evaluating—and list *specific behaviors* of the counselor that you would associate with each phase. Share these lists in class and compile a single master list.
   Rationale: Cooperative learning strategies such as this allow students to reach beyond the text and class lectures. Many good ideas can come from this type of activity.

4. Interview a classroom teacher about his or her perspectives on counseling services in schools. What degree of input should teachers have in designing a counseling program? What role does the teacher have in a comprehensive program?
   Rationale: Successful school counselors collaborate with their teaching colleagues. Understanding teachers' perceptions about

school counseling services is an initial step in developing collaborative efforts.

Test Questions

(b)   1. According to the textbook, a comprehensive school counseling program
   (a) is more effective than services in private practice.
   (b) is a planned component of the larger school purpose and mission.
   (c) includes medical services for all students.
   (d) is a new term for classroom developmental guidance programs.

(a)   2. The primary purpose for comprehensive school counseling programs is to assist with
   (a) the educational, career, personal and social development of students.
   (b) test administration and identification of exceptional students.
   (c) family counseling services and referrals to community agencies.
   (d) school discipline by helping students improve their behavior.

(c)   3. Planning, Organizing, Implementing, and Evaluating are four phases of
   (a) classroom guidance,
   (b) individual counseling,
   (c) a comprehensive counseling program,
   (d) parent education programs.

(b)   4. An important part of program planning for school counseling is
   (a) performance appraisal,
   (b) needs assessment,
   (c) professional development activities,
   (d) evaluation of counseling services.

(a)   5. A guidance curriculum is usually
   (a) a guide for teachers to integrate guidance into daily instruction.
   (b) a manual that counselors must use in doing classroom guidance.
   (c) the result of a law that says schools must have guidance.
   (d) mandated for all teachers in all grade levels.

__(b)__   6. Everything educational that is done by teachers, administrators, counselor and others can be related to the concept of
(a) Progressive Education.
(b) guiding students.
(c) discipline.
(d) self-directed learning.

__(d)__   7. Developmental counseling is
(a) an approach that uses Maslow's hierarchy of needs.
(b) the antithesis to behavioral therapy.
(c) a euphemism for play therapy.
(d) designed to help students develop skills to reach healthy life goals.

__(a)__   8. A counselor's Advisory Committee
(a) helps guide the planning and development of a comprehensive program.
(b) alerts the principal to problems in the counseling program.
(c) takes the place of an assistant principal.
(d) determines which students should receive warnings each grading period.

__(c)__   9. Not all experts agree that career, educational, and social/personal development should define comprehensive counseling programs because these aspects are
(a) too liberal in design.
(b) misunderstood concepts by most teachers.
(c) responsible for the fragmented role of the school counselor.
(d) too academically oriented.

__(b)__   10. Ideally, school counseling centers should
(a) be located as far away from the principals office as possible.
(b) have ample space to provide the essential services of a comprehensive program.
(c) have private restrooms for the counselor.
(d) be located away from the flow of traffic in the school.

Matching Items

COLUMN A	COLUMN B
(c) Alfred Adler	A. Providing services
(b) Career Night	B. School-wide guidance
(e) Planning	C. Life tasks: work, sharing with others, and loving relationship
(a) Implementing	D. Program evaluation
(d) Accountability	E. First phase of a counseling program

Chapter 3

The School Counselor

OBJECTIVES

(1) Provide a general overview of similarities and differences of school counselors across the three levels of practice
(2) Indicate how school counselors interact with parents and teachers.
(3) Highlight certification issues at state and national levels.
(4) Examine national training standards for professional counselors.

CHAPTER SUMMARY

This chapter examines the various roles, training, and credentials of counselors at all levels of school service. The roles of elementary, middle, and high school counselors are presented with emphasis on counseling services for students and involvement of parents and teachers. The second part of the chapter discusses aspects of training for professional counselors especially standards by the National Board of Certified Counselors (NBCC) and the Council for Accreditation of Counseling and Related Educational Programs (CACREP). The final section examines certification issues for school counselors.

KEY CONCEPTS, EVENTS, NAMES, AND TERMS

Concepts and Events

• *Elementary and Secondary Education Act of 1965*
• *Education for All Handicapped Children Act of 1975*
• *A Nation at Risk* report
• Child and adolescent counseling
• Parental involvement
• Guidance curriculum

Names

• *Guidance in the Curriculum* (ASCD), 1955
• NCATE
• NBCC
• CACREP

Terms

• Developmental counseling
• Teacher-Advisee Program
• Information services
• Transitional services

21

Varying Roles of School Counselors

In most instances, school counselors use the same basic helping processes—counseling, consulting, coordinating, and appraising—across all the school years. The role and functions of school counselors are influenced by both the specific level of practice and the needs of particular school populations being served.

The Elementary School Counselor

The 1960s saw an emergence of counseling in elementary schools brought about by events such as the publication of the *Elementary School Guidance and Counseling* journal, inclusion of elementary officers in the American School Counselor Association, enactment of the Elementary and Secondary Education Act of 1965 (ESEA), and the extension of the NDEA Act in 1965, which provided funds for training institutes in elementary guidance and counseling.

The 1970s and 1980s saw increased attention on services to elementary children. Understandably, this increased demand for elementary counseling brought with it the urgency to define and describe what an ideal elementary counseling program should include.

Counseling Children

Successful individual counseling with young children depends on the accurate assessment of the child's readiness for this type of relationship. Counselors assess a child's language development, behavior, cognitive functioning, and ability to understand the nature and purpose of a helping relationship.

Group work with children is an important vehicle that counselors use to facilitate children's interaction with others and an exploration of their perceptions within a social context. Group work in elementary schools is most often structured as group guidance or group counseling.

Developmental Counseling

The assumption made by elementary counselors is that children become successful when allowed to achieve sequential goals that lead them towards self-fulfillment. As such, developmental counseling considers the stages of child development, including important life tasks that all children must learn and accomplish in moving toward the next level of functioning.

Parental Involvement

Elementary counselors rely heavily on parental involvement in helping children plan and achieve developmental goals (Note: The terms *parent* and *parental involvement* refer to all forms of parental and guardian relationships.).

Teacher Involvement

To establish effective services in elementary schools, counselors develop strong working relationships with teachers and other school personnel. Elementary teachers become actively involved in the school counseling program through the guidance activities they integrate in daily instruction. School counselors have an important role to play in encouraging their schools and teachers to integrate guidance, and that role is addressed throughout this book.

Another area of teacher involvement in elementary counseling is in fostering parent-school relationships.

Finally, teachers who have expertise in areas of child development and instruction are vital resources for staff development.

The Middle School Counselor

A first step for counselors who accept the challenge of a middle school program is to define their counseling role with the pre-adolescent student.

Counseling Pre-Adolescents

Counseling middle-graders requires expanded approaches that include individual helping relationships, group experiences, peer support systems, and other processes.

Group processes are of particular value in middle school counseling programs because of the desire of this age student to be a part of a group; to belong and to be accepted.

Group and individual relationships are also useful in establishing effective peer helper programs, which have become a focal point for middle school counseling services.

Transitional Services

Middle school counselors provide many services that enable students to make smooth transitions from their childhood years to adolescence.

As with elementary counseling, a key to establishing successful middle school services is the involvement of teachers.

Teacher Involvement

A comprehensive middle school counseling program reflects the mission of the school, helping teachers create and deliver appropriate instruction for all students, encouraging group processes such as instructional teams and advisory groups, and becoming part of the school's leadership team.

Counseling programs that are built around teacher involvement usually offer some type of advisor-advisee service, which is particularly helpful with middle school development. Successful teacher-advisee programs usually have strong counselor involvement.

Parental Involvement

Because parents of middle-graders struggle themselves with entry into this transitional period, programs that assist parents with their feelings and skill development are appropriate.

The High School Counselor

Although the present-day high school counselor's role is changing, the typical secondary counselor continues to assist students by providing information about course selections, career opportunities, test results, colleges, and scholarships.

Counseling and Guiding Adolescents

Adolescents continue to need services that are developmental in nature, focusing on educational and career planning, academic achievement, social acceptance, self-awareness, sexual development, and other factors. Yet, many of their specific concerns are more problem-centered and crisis-oriented than simply developmental in nature.

Group procedures are notably infrequent in high school counseling programs for both group counseling and group guidance activities.

Career Planning And Decision-Making

Studies of the high school counselor's role indicate that career planning is a vital component of secondary programs.

Information Services

Beyond the major functions of counseling, consulting, and appraising performed by high school counselors, another vital service is coordinating information for students, parents, and teachers. How counselors choose to disseminate information, the processes used to ensure that all students have equal opportunity to receive accurate information, is fundamental to a comprehensive high school counseling program.

Parent/Teacher Involvement
High school years are signified by increased independence and responsibility for most students. However, the increasing importance of post-secondary education has extended the need for parental involvement.

Some high schools have adapted the teacher as advisor program (TAP), and have seen positive effects on important criteria, such as school attendance, that relate to student success in school.

What these trends tell us is that future high school counseling programs may need to encourage more parent and teacher involvement than has been expected in the past.

Training of School Counselors

Because there are no consistent guidelines mandated for training school counselors, we find a wide variance in requirements across the 50 states.

At the national level in recent years, the counseling profession has promoted standards through the National Board for Certified Counselors (NBCC) and the Council for the Accreditation of Counseling and Related Educational Programs (CACREP).

As the school counseling profession continues to address issues related to its growth and development, the training standards for educational counselors will continue to need review.

The Helping Relationship

The role of school counselors is influenced by the theoretical models and clinical techniques adapted and applied by counselors in their individual schools.

Counseling Theories and Approaches
Forming helping relationships with students, parents, and teachers in school settings may use different theoretical perspectives, that depend on the theoretical orientation of the counselor and needs of clients.

Communication Skills
Optimal use of helping processes requires a command of basic communication skills. The training of school counselors consists of course work and practice in listening, facilitating, and decision-making skills.

The Process of Helping
Counseling, as used here, is not advice giving. Rather, it is the process of helping people examine concerns, gather necessary information, explore possibilities, and formulate plans of action.

Counseling is more than having conversations with students who need assistance. It is movement from the identification of a concern to the implementation of a strategy to address important life goals.

Human Development

A second area of study for school counselors is human development. This area frequently includes courses in developmental and abnormal psychology, sociology, family relations, and learning theory.

Knowledge of Behavioral Science
Understanding different theories of behavioral development complements the various counseling approaches used in forming effective helping relationships.

A Life-span Approach
Counselors who work in schools need an appreciation of the life-span of human development theory. Because school counselors work with audiences from all levels, children through adulthood, they require an understanding of where each person is in his or her development.

Group Processes

Because schools employ only a few counselors to meet the needs of many students, group skills are essential in providing counseling, informational, and instructional services. School counselors use these skills with three types of groups: group counseling, group guidance, and group consultation.

Group Counseling
As with individual counseling, group counseling forms a confidential relationship in which students explore concerns and establish plans of action. Group counseling offers the added dimension of encouraging students to help one another.

Group Guidance

Group skills learned in counselor education programs are useful in providing instructional and informational services. Counselors need these skills for classroom presentations and use them in other educational activities such as parent education programs, financial aid workshops, and other large group activities.

Group Consultation

Sometimes students can best be assisted if the counselor consults with all the adults who are relating with these students. Group consultations with teachers and other professionals require special understanding of consulting relationships, roles, and communication skills.

Student Appraisal

Assessing students and environments are two more functions of school counselors that require specific training in test theory, development, and application. A strong background in tests and measurement ensures the appropriate use and interpretation of data gathering instruments and processes.

Formal Assessment

Testing and using other instruments to gather data about students and their environments are types of formal assessment processes.

Informal Assessment

School counselors are trained in informal assessment procedures, which include observation techniques, life-style questionnaires, and the use of art, play, or other activity to collect data and form diagnoses about situations.

Career Development Theory and Information

To choose appropriate strategies in helping students address career issues, school counselors receive training in career development theories and information services.

Knowledge and implementation of information services are important to counselors, especially secondary counselors, in helping students have the most recent and up-to-date information about career trends and educational requirements.

Educational Research

Effective school counselors demonstrate that the services they provide to students, parents, and teachers make a difference in students' development and in the life of the school. To accept this responsibility and actively design processes for evaluating services, counselors must have a basic understanding of research techniques.

Social and Cultural Foundations

Schools in the United States today serve divergent populations and every indication is that this trend will continue for years to come. When counselor education programs provide information about the structural, sociological, and cultural changes in society, and explore expected outcomes and trends related to these developments, they place their graduates in a stronger position to help schools deliver needed services to students, parents and teachers.

Changing Society

Counselors who are familiar with societal changes and their impact on human development are better equipped to help students and teachers deal with the present consequences of these events, and to predict future trends.

Multicultural Populations

Counselors who are sensitive to ethnic and racial differences and willingly celebrate the cultural diversity of their communities are able to form beneficial relationships with a broad spectrum of people.

Ethical and Legal Issues

School counselors must know the ethical principles put forth by their profession, and balance that understanding with a clear knowledge of local policies, state statutes, and federal laws relating to the practice of counseling in schools.

The School Setting

In addition to the above areas of study, school counselors also learn about the nature of educational institutions and, specifically, the practice of counseling in a school setting.

Credentials of School Counselors

Since the 1970s, credentialing of counselors has become a major issue in the profession.

In addition to certification and licensure, the counseling profession has worked to create accreditation processes for institutions that train counselors.

The National Council for Accreditation of Teacher Education (NCATE) is the most common accrediting body for teacher education and related training programs in departments and schools of education at colleges and universities. The Council for Accreditation of Counseling and Related Programs (CACREP) reviews and approves training programs for counselors who are being prepared to work in a variety of settings, including schools.

State Certification

To practice as a school counselor, the first credential one must receive is state certification (sometimes called licensure). All states require certification and the vast majority require a minimum of a master's degree for initial certification. Several states continue to require teaching experience as a prerequisite to counselor employment despite the absence of research showing that such experience relates to effective school counseling.

National Certification

In the 1980s the American Counseling Association (ACA), became active in establishing a national certification process for professional counselors. A National Board for Certified Counselors (NBCC) was established and an application, review, and examination process was created. The NBCC has also established specialty exams and certifications in career, gerontological, and school counseling.

All these certification and credentialing processes, at state, regional, and national levels aim at improving the identification and performance of practicing counselors.

The description the school counselor's role advocated in this chapter integrates the essential services of a comprehensive counseling program across all levels of school practice.

Exercises

1. In a brief research project, investigate the historical development of another helping profession (e.g., nursing, medicine, psychology, social work) and compare your findings with the counseling profession. How did these other professions begin? What route did their credentialing processes take to reach the point where they are today?

   Rationale: Comparisons with the development of other helping professions help students more clearly identify differences and similarities with the counseling profession.

2. In a small group, discuss the issue of integrating guidance in the school curriculum. Highlight some of the points made in this text and contrast them with other views. Have your group take a position and outline three to five reasons you are taking this stand. Share your conclusions with the class.

   Rationale: Without an integration of guidance into the curriculum a comprehensive counseling program may be unattainable. Having students practice conveying their views about this issue gives them experience with which to convince their teaching colleagues is the future.

3. A school principal interviews you for a high school counseling position. She was an elementary principal before coming to the high school and says that she would like the high school program to reflect the philosophy of elementary counseling. How would you respond?

   Rationale: This text adheres to the belief that there are more common traits among elementary, middle and high school counseling programs than there are differences that distinguish them.

4. You are a new counselor at a middle school that serves a community with diverse cultures. List some steps you would take to prepare yourself to be an effective counselor with students who come from diverse backgrounds.

   Rationale: Practicing one's philosophy about cultural diversity and having it critiqued in a safe environment, such as a graduate class, is an important experience for all professional counselors.

Test Questions

Multiple Choice Items

(b)   1. In general, high school counselors
(a) use more group procedures than elementary or middle
school counselors,
(b) use fewer group procedures than elementary or middle
school counselors,
(c) see fewer students than either elementary or middle school
counselors,
(d) do more teacher consultation than elementary counselors

(a)   2. The text in this course takes the position that
comprehensive counseling programs at the elementary,
middle, and high school levels
(a) are similar because the essential major functions of school
counselors are similar,
(b) are totally different because of the needs of students and
these three levels,
(c) cannot be compared because they are so different,
(d) should be identical because they all work with students,
parents, and teachers.

(c)   3. In assessing children's potential to be successful in
counseling relationships, counselors assess students'
(a) academic achievement.
(b) socio-economic status.
(c) behavioral and cognitive development.
(d) psycho-somatic history.

(b)   4. In developmental programs, the goals of a guidance
curriculum are linked to
(a) a student's academic record.
(b) the therapeutic goals of counseling services.
(c) parental consent.
(d) legislative mandates for character education.

(b)   5. Parental involvement in schools
(a) is not an area of concern for counselors.
(b) has been related to higher student success in school.
(c) should be discouraged if professionals are to maintain
control of our schools.
(d) is not as important in the upper grades as it is in
elementary schools.

<u>(c)</u>   6. Some studies indicate that high school counselors
      (a) are less prepared than elementary and middle school
         counselors.
      (b) do more group counseling than other counselors.
      (c) spend too much time in clerical and administrative tasks.
      (d) should have doctoral degrees in counseling.

<u>(b)</u>   7. Career planning is a vital service of
      (a) elementary teachers and counselors.
      (b) high school counselors.
      (c) special education teachers.
      (d) Advisory Committees.

<u>(a)</u>   8. Parental involvement at the high school level
      (a) seems to be increasingly important in U.S. society.
      (b) is unnecessary unless there is some specific need or
         problem.
      (c) should be discouraged to enhance students' independence.
      (d) has minimal effect on the success of students.

<u>(d)</u>   9. Many states require teaching experience to become a school
         counselor
      (a) unless the counselor has a degree in psychology.
      (b) unless the counselor is an NCC.
      (c) proving that there is a strong relationship between
         counseling and teaching.
      (d) even though no research supports a relationship
         between teaching experience and a counselor's
         effectiveness.

<u>(b)</u>   10. The National Board of Certified Counselors (NBCC)
      (a) is a division of the American Counseling Association.
      (b) recommends eight areas of knowledge as the core base for
         all specialties in the counseling profession.
      (c) is affiliated with the American Psychological Association.
      (d) only certifies mental health counselors.

Matching Items

(b)	NBCC	A. Report about low achievement of students in U.S.
(a)	*A Nation at Risk*	
(d)	*Guidance in the Curriculum*	
(e)	CACREP	B. Certification Board
(c)	NCATE	C. Accrediting body for teachers
		D. ASCD Annual
		E. Accrediting body for counselors

Chapter 4

Essential Services

OBJECTIVES

1) Describe the major functions performed by school counselors in a comprehensive program of services.
2) Illustrate how these functions are used to serve students, parents, and teachers.
3) Examine the various ways that school counselors coordinate services for students.

CHAPTER SUMMARY

In the past, school counseling programs focused primarily on the development of individual students and offered services that typically emphasized one-to-one relationships. A comprehensive school counseling program consists of a wide range of services to address students, parents, and teachers' needs. Contemporary school counseling services are essential to a school's educational mission. This chapter is a summary of how counselors integrate these essential services into a comprehensive program. These services are listed under the broad categories: *counseling, consulting, coordinating, and appraising.*

KEY CONCEPTS, EVENTS, NAMES, AND TERMS

Concepts and Events

- Cognitive development
- Triangular relationship
- Individual student planning
- School climate
- Family Educational Rights and Privacy Act of 1974
- Referrals
- Family assessment

Names

- Verne Faust
- Public Law 94-142
- Buckley Amendment

Terms

- Counseling
- Consulting
- Classroom guidance
- Student Services Team
- Guidance curriculum
- Coordinating
- Teacher-Advisee Program
- Peer Helper Program
- Appraising

35

Counseling

This section focuses on what counseling is and how elementary, middle, and senior high school counselors use this process with students, parents, and teachers.

Individual Counseling

School counselors spend a significant amount of time working with individual students to help them focus on particular concerns and make decisions about their goals, relationships, and self-development.

Behavioral maturity and cognitive development are two more areas that complement a student's verbal skills to make individual counseling successful.

In schools where counselors are responsible for a large number of students, the decision of whether or not to use individual counseling is related to the time available.

Group Counseling

By establishing groups, counselors use common concerns as a basis for counseling, solicit the support and assistance of each group member, ask members to focus on their major concerns, and thereby reach a greater number of students

In comprehensive school counseling programs, group counseling is an essential service, and to include it, counselors seek suggestions from teachers and administrators to design reasonable schedules without significantly disrupting the instructional program.

Student Counseling

Students are challenged by critical issues that affect their personal, social, educational, and career development. It is essential that counselors schedule time for individual and group counseling relationships.

Because comprehensive school counseling programs have a broad focus and serve a wide range of students' needs, counselors try to keep their counseling relationships brief.

Parent and Teacher Counseling

Sometimes school counselors are approached by parents and teachers who disclose their own personal problems. The first question school counselors ask themselves in situations such as this is: Should I be providing this service in the counseling program? No clear consensus exists among professional school counselors regarding this question. School counselors take each situation as it develops and use their best ethical and professional judgment to provide appropriate services.

Consulting

School counselors frequently receive requests for services that do not require direct counseling.

Two criteria make consulting different from counseling: (1) Consulting establishes a triangular relationship including the consultant, consultee, and an external situation usually involving a third individual or a group of people; and (2) Consulting services often use *indirect helping processes* to address an identified situation.

The focus of consultation is a specific need or situation for which information, instruction, or facilitation are requested by a student, parent, or teacher. By using a variety of consulting services, counselors disseminate information, instruct groups, lead teacher-parent conferences, and plan other services to help a large number of students in schools.

Information Services

School counselors often act as resources for information needed by students, parents, and teachers.

Community and School Resources
As a resource in the school, the counselor is available to help parents and teachers locate information in the school system and community to assist with children's total development.

Career Opportunities
In elementary and middle schools, counselors provide information to students and teachers about the world of work and career opportunities to help with early career exploration. Usually, counselors and teachers use this information to design career guidance experiences that they integrate with classroom instruction.

At all school levels, the media center is a vital resource center for a wide range of materials including career information.

Educational Opportunities
Another type of informational consultation is when counselors locate educational services, programs, and opportunities that complement and support students' overall development.

At the senior high school, educational consultation becomes more visible as an essential service of the school counseling program.

Financial Assistance
School counselors are frequent providers of information regarding financial resources for families and their children. For some students, financial assistance can make the difference in meeting basic clothing and nourishment needs so they can adequately learn in school.

In high schools, counselors help adolescents with resources to meet their basic needs, and also help families find the funds for appropriate post-secondary opportunities.

Instructional Services

Contemporary school counselors include large group instruction as part of their consulting services for students, parents, and teachers. These instructional relationships are similar to classroom instruction in that they impart information or teach new skills, but they also are different because they are free of evaluative appearances.

Classroom Guidance
Comprehensive school counseling programs include large group services as well as individual counseling to meet the unique needs of students. Guidance is an essential area of the curriculum, and teachers and counselors collaborate to plan effective guidance activities in the daily instruction.

In comprehensive programs, counselors also use guidance instruction in small group sessions. Sometimes, the difference between ongoing small group guidance and group counseling becomes blurred.

Parent Education
By using their consulting skills and instructing parents in various aspects of child development, adolescent behavior, and communication skills, school counselors provide indirect services to a larger number of students.

Teacher In-service

A third type of instructional format used by school counselors is teacher in-service workshops.

Problem-Solving Services

Counselors use consulting skills and processes to assist people in resolving conflicts, accepting the views of others, and selecting agreeable goals to move forward.

Parent-Teacher Conferences

One way that school counselors assume a consulting role to resolve problems is by facilitating parent-teacher conferences. The role of the counselor in these conferences varies depending on the issues at hand and the person who has initiated the conference.

Administrative Conferences

Another situation in which school counselors use their consulting skills is when principals and other administrators seek information about problems with particular students, or difficulties they observe in the school as a whole. Communication between administrators and counselors is essential to provide appropriate and comprehensive services in schools.

Student Services Team Conferences

Generally, these teams include the school counselor, a psychologist, a social worker, a nurse, an administrator, and teachers, with special education teachers usually represented. Occasionally, these teams include professionals from agencies outside the school. The main purpose of student services teams is to follow cases of children and adolescents who are experiencing particular learning and behavioral difficulties.

Other School Services

In addition to establishing consulting relationships to disseminate information, give instruction, and facilitate conferences, school counselors assist schools in planning school-wide activities.

Guidance Curriculum

Guidance is the responsibility of everyone in the school and is best implemented when integrated as an essential part of the curriculum. Guidance does not occur at a single moment or as a solitary event. Rather, it is infused with all subjects, and in all daily instruction.

Individual Student Planning

Adequate and appropriate services for students require conscious and careful planning. Some students struggle with serious concerns that demand attention beyond participation in guidance and educational programs. These students need more intense preventive and remedial services.

School Climate

In planning healthy school climates, counselors help administrators and teachers evaluate programs that enhance learning and they determine whether these programs accomplish what is intended. Counselors also ask administrators to assess physical aspects of schools, and review school policies to determine if they contribute to healthy environments.

Special Events and Projects

Many events in elementary, middle, and high schools supplement instructional programs during the year. Counselors who plan events such as "Substance Abuse Awareness Week," "Good Citizen of the Month Award," and "Special Olympics" illustrate their commitment to the school and student development.

Coordinating

Counselors deliver many services and have responsibility for coordinating a number of other activities that benefit students and schools.

Data Collection and Sharing

Throughout students' educational careers, schools gather information to help teachers make accurate decisions about student learning. School counselors are trained to assist teachers in collecting data to make these important decisions.

Test Administration

Tests are generally used to determine students' aptitude and achievement in school. Counselors administer individual and group tests and other assessment instruments if the need for information exists.

Test Results

Appropriate distribution and utilization of test data require adequate coordination. Again, school counselors have the training to help students, parents, and teachers understand test data, and consequently to use these results in making educational and career decisions.

School counselors can assist teachers in selecting appropriate evaluative processes and instruments, and in using the data collected to improve instruction and student learning.

The major point is that counselors are trained in testing and measurement techniques, and they not only use this training to administer tests and inventories but also to coordinate the use of data from these assessment instruments.

Students' Records

Decisions about what information should be placed in students' cumulative folders are guided by local policies, state regulations, and federal laws. A major guide for schools is the Family Educational Rights and Privacy Act, commonly called the Buckley Amendment, passed by Congress in 1974.

Referrals and Follow-up

Occasionally, a social, psychological, financial, or other factor hinders a student's progress in school and the school cannot address these obstacles adequately without assistance from others. School counselors are the logical choice among school staff members to coordinate and follow-up these referrals.

Community Agencies

Several public and private agencies offer services to children, adolescents, and families. School counselors, as coordinators of referrals for their schools, attempt to gather current information about these resources so that students, parents, and teachers can make the best decisions about services outside the school.

Private Practitioners

In addition to public agencies and programs, most communities have private practitioners and institutions that offer services for children and families. School counselors coordinate referrals to private resources in the same way that they work with public agencies.

School-Wide Events

These activities are either part of ongoing programs, or they are special events planned to address particular developmental needs of students. The following ideas are a few school-wide events and programs for which counselors might assume some responsibility.

Student Recognition Activities

Career Awareness Programs

Teacher-Advisee Programs

Peer Helper Programs

The preceding examples illustrate activities that help counselors and teachers reach a higher percentage of students.

Appraising

Since the beginning of the school counseling profession, counselors have used appraisal instruments and assessment processes to measure students' needs, interests, intellectual functions, and academic performance.

Student Evaluation

Tests are among the most common assessment instruments used by school counselors.

Tests

Evaluation through standardized testing has been and will continue to be an important service of school counseling programs.

Inventories

School counselors use a variety of questionnaires and inventories to assist students with educational and career decisions.

Observations and Interviews

School counselors use direct observations and interviews to gather relevant data. In addition, counselors interview teachers, parents, and students as part of the evaluation process. Students' records provide an added source of information about past events and academic progress that assist in evaluation and decision-making processes.

Group Assessment

There are two major types of group tests used in measuring student achievement: criterion-referenced and norm-referenced instruments. Further description of these types of standardized tests is presented in Chapter 8.

Some school counselors and teachers also apply Sociometric techniques in assessing students' roles and relationships in groups.

Environmental Evaluation

A third area of appraising centers on environmental factors that influence students' development and learning.

Assessment of School Climate

By creating appraisal processes to help teachers and administrators assess school environments, counselors gather data with which to plan efficient and effective services. Altering negative aspects of a school is the first step in creating healthy environments and encouraging students to learn.

Assessment of Families

By assessing home environments, counselors determine the level of support a student is receiving from his or her family structure, and use this information to seek appropriate community services.

Peer Group Assessment

A final aspect of environmental evaluation that contributes to the overall student appraisal is the assessment of social peer groups. Many of the methods already discussed are useful for assessing peer relationships. In particular, structured interviews and observations are viable assessment techniques.

In this chapter, we have examined the four essential services of a school counseling program: counseling, consulting, coordinating, and appraising. These four services form distinct categories that together identify a broad role for professional counselors in schools.

Exercises

1. Brainstorm by yourself about factors that influence how much time school counselors choose to spend in a particular service area. List these factors and share them in class. In the class discussion, come to consensus about the three most influential factors. Which, if any, of these factors can be controlled by the counselor? Discuss what your findings mean to the role of a school counselor.
   Rationale: In comprehensive programs, time management is essential. For students to learn how to manage their time efficiently, they may benefit from exploring the most influential factors that affect a counselor's time.

2. A curriculum supervisor in the school system reports to your principal that counselors should not see students in individual counseling for more than four sessions because to do so would be considered "therapy," and counselors are not therapists. Discuss in a small group how you would respond to this situation. Highlight the main points of your discussion with the class.
   Rationale: Historically there has been a debate among school counselors and other professionals about the role of individual counseling in school programs. This exercise encourages students to clarify their own views on this issue.

3. As a school counselor, you might spend considerable time coordinating services for students. This could mean spending time on the phone with agencies, meeting with parents, completing appropriate referral forms, and other functions that go unnoticed by your fellow teachers. Such "invisible" functioning risks criticism from teachers who might say, "I don't ever see the counselor, and don't know what the counselor does." What are some active measures you could take as a counselor to keep your teaching colleagues informed about what you do regarding referrals?
   Rationale: School counselors are continually questioned about their role and purpose. Students need to have practical ideas that will help them keep their counseling program and services visible in their schools. This relates to the "public relations" role of the school counselor.

4. Create a brochure or flier about a counseling program that illustrates or describes the essential services provided. What factors are most important to consider as you design this brochure?
   Rationale: School counselors should take control of their role and disseminating information through brochures and fliers is one strategy to use. Designing information that is attractive and readable to the intended audience is important to the success of such vehicles.

Test Questions

Multiple Choice Items

__(b)__   1. Because individual counseling relies to a great extent on the verbal skills of both the counselor and client, it is
   (a) the most important service offered by school counselors.
   (b) not an appropriate service for every student.
   (c) best left to school psychologists.
   (d) only effective with students in middle grades and above.

__(d)__   2. The decision of whether of not to use individual counseling in a school counseling program is related, in part, to the
   (a) counselor's certification level.
   (b) teacher's approval.
   (c) student's social status.
   (d) time available to provide this service.

__(b)__   3. One factor that guides a school counselor's decision to refer a student to another professional for counseling is
   (a) permission from the school principal.
   (b) the counselor's knowledge and training in the specific area of concern.
   (c) an Advisory Committee's recommendation.
   (d) the student's academic achievement.

__(c)__   4. School counselors who provide counseling services to parents and teachers
   (a) are practicing unethically and should be reported to their professional association.
   (b) should discontinue such service, because school policies usually forbid this practice.
   (c) use their best professional judgment to determine if they are the appropriate person to provide these services.
   (d) should consult with their principals about these cases.

__(b)__   5. The differences between counseling and therapy
   (a) have been clearly delineated in literature and research.
   (b) are still debated among helping professionals.
   (c) are the same as the differences between education and counseling.
   (d) are only important when considering school counseling.

<u>(a)</u>   6. Consulting relationships for counselors in schools include
        problem-solving, informational, and
     (a) instructional situations,
     (b) therapeutic conditions,
     (c) profit-making arrangements,
     (d) administrative duties.

<u>(b)</u>   7. Informational services can include information about
        community resources, career and educational
        opportunities, and
     (a) problems discussed with students in counseling.
     (b) financial assistance sought by students for college.
     (c) a teacher's effectiveness in classroom instruction.
     (d) students' views about teacher performance.

<u>(c)</u>   8. Classroom guidance, parent education programs, and
        teacher workshops are
     (a) usually not effective use of a counselor's time.
     (b) the most important functions of a school counselor.
     (c) examples of instructional consultation.
     (d) not generally found in comprehensive programs.

<u>(a)</u>   9. A major guide to help schools use students' records
        appropriately is the
     (a) Family Educational Rights and Privacy Act of 1974.
     (b) *Record Keeping Annual* of the National Principals'
        Association.
     (c) ruling of the *Tarasoff Case* in California.
     (d) *Counselor's Handbook of Record Keeping* by the
        American School Counselor Association.

<u>(d)</u>   10. A key ingredient of successful teacher-advisee programs is
     (a) a counselor's role as a substitute in the classroom so
        teachers can advise students.
     (b) students' training as advisees.
     (c) the parents' role as volunteers.
     (d) the training of teachers in helping skills.

Matching Items

COLUMN A

(i)	financial assistance
(h)	group consultation
(f)	classroom guidance
(j)	parent conference
(e)	Student Services Team
(a)	Buckley Amendment
(g)	Teacher-Advisee Program
(d)	peer helper
(b)	group counseling
(c)	consulting

COLUMN B

A. about student records
B. a confidential process
C. an indirect helping process
D. a student
E. school counseling, nursing, social work and psychological services
F. best when integrated into the curriculum
G. teachers meet regularly with same students
H. useful in disseminating information or instructing
I. e.g., contacting Social Services for food stamps
J. seeks involvement

47

Chapter 5

Developing a Comprehensive Program

OBJECTIVEs

*1) Present phases and steps for developing comprehensive
counseling services in schools.*
*2) Illustrate how counselors seek administrator and teachers'
support for services.*
*3. Show how counselors and teachers determine assignments
within a comprehensive program of services.*
*4) Offer suggestions of how counselors might manage time in
providing a broad array of services.*

CHAPTER SUMMARY

This chapter offers some of the practical aspects of putting together
a comprehensive program of counseling, consulting, and coordinating
services in a school setting. These aspects are, of necessity, presented in
a general nature, and are applicable across all levels—elementary
through high school—of school counseling programs.

KEY CONCEPTS, NAMES, AND TERMS

Concepts

- Annual plan
- Assessing needs
- Learning-related goals
- Service-related goals
- Marketing the Program
- Balancing time
- Scheduling

Terms

- Counseling
- Consulting
- Coordinating
- Advisory Committee
- Appraising
- Evaluating

CHAPTER SYNOPSIS

In this chapter, we use the four phases of designing a
comprehensive program presented in Chapter 2 as major headings—
planning, organizing, implementing, and evaluating. Practical
considerations include: assessing the current program, seeking input
and support for change, assessing the needs of students, parents, and
teachers, determining resources, assigning responsibilities, marketing
the program, scheduling services, balancing time, providing services,

and evaluating outcomes. The last of these, dealing with program evaluation, is introduced for practical consideration here, but is more thoroughly presented later in Chapter 10.

Planning

One of the first steps in planning a comprehensive counseling program is to determine what has existed in prior years. This is particularly important for a new counselor coming into a school situation where there has been a program of services in the past.

Assessing the Current Program

A first step in formulating this plan is to determine the breadth of services in prior years. This means gathering data about what services were provided, how program decisions were made, what processes were used to evaluate services, and how people perceived the counseling program.

In addition to asking the principal and teachers about their perceptions, counselors might use surveys and interviews with parents and students to provide useful information for examining the counseling program. After the counselor is satisfied that crucial elements of the program have been identified for possible change, a next step is to involve people in the decision-making process.

Seeking Input and Support for Change

By definition, a comprehensive school counseling program is planned as part of an inclusive process. This means that the program does not belong to any single professional, nor is it the sole responsibility of the school counselor. By including as many people as possible in program planning, counselors are likely to have widespread support for their services.

The first person to include is the building principal. Understanding how the principal perceives counseling services in the school, and learning that the principal may be willing to adopt new perceptions about program areas is important.

One medium that can facilitate this exchange of information is an Advisory Committee. An Advisory Committee of a school counseling program is a vehicle counselors use to obtain input from teachers, administrators, parents, and students about appropriate services and activities.

Another reason school counselors seek suggestions from students, parents, and teachers is to supplement the findings of the needs' assessment process. Typically, surveys of students, parents, and teachers will discover some critical concerns and needs of students in the school.

Assessing Students', Parents', and Teachers' Needs

In determining what goals and objectives to include in a comprehensive school counseling program, first counselors investigate the needs of the populations to be served. One way that counselors collect needs' assessment data is through surveys with students, parents, and teachers. Forms 5.1, 5.2, and 5.3 illustrate sample assessment surveys for students, parents, and teachers. The survey form for students is designed for middle graders (5.1), the parent form is for elementary schools (5.2), and the teacher form for high schools (5.3).

As noted earlier, needs assessments can be done by using methods of data collection other than surveys. For example, counselors might interview students, parents, and teachers, or they might simply observe in the school and community and draw conclusions from these observations. In some instances, counselors might use the results of their annual program evaluation as an assessment procedure.

Determining Resources

When speaking of resources for a school counseling program, we usually refer to people as the primary resource. A comprehensive program also benefits from the materials, equipment, and space available to the counselor, but without adequate human support all these other elements will make little difference.

Successful school counselors are adept at learning about the talents of their teaching colleagues and are creative in soliciting support from other personnel. Successful counselors learn about the services and resources of the communities and states in which their schools reside.

Comprehensive programs also consist of adequate materials, equipment, and space to do the job.

To create programs that maintain a realistic vision, counselors assess school needs, interpret these data accurately, and determine what resources are available to provide the most effective and efficient services. This is why needs assessment processes are important and can help schools set goals for the counseling program, which moves us to the next phase of comprehensive program development—organizing.

Organizing

Successful counseling programs tend to have several things in common, but most important among the key elements is that the services of counselors are organized as an integral and essential part of the broader school mission. In organizing their programs, counselors attempt to set goals that address the identified needs of students, parents, and teachers.

Setting Goals

In setting goals, the counselor summarizes data from surveys, interviews, observations, and other assessment processes, and presents results to the Advisory Committee. Figure 5.1 in the text illustrates a sample planning sheet used by a middle school counselor to identify students' needs and recommend program goals to classroom teachers.

Some goals are set as a result of local and state mandates and standards that aim at providing equal services to all students. All these goals, those set as a result of students' needs assessments and those mandated by the state, become part of a school plan to meet the developmental needs of students.

Learning-Related Goals

In some cases, selected goals relate directly to an identified need. For example, if a high school survey finds that students need to associate their educational success with future career satisfaction, a goal might be: To increase student awareness of the significant correlation between educational achievement and career development. Such a goal would be a learning-related one for all students.

Service-Related Goals

Sometimes goals indirectly address the expressed needs of students, parents, and teachers. For example, to address career awareness the goal might be: To increase the number of career guidance sessions with eighth-grade students.

Goals can take different forms and be addressed through a variety of services and activities.

Assigning Responsibilities

A well-organized school counseling program not only identifies important goals, but also assigns who is responsible for providing services and activities to address the intended objectives.

Activities that are incorporated into the curriculum, such as developmental guidance, are the primary responsibility of classroom teachers. Sometimes, counselors share this responsibility by co-leading certain guidance lessons with teachers, or they might assume total responsibility for presenting a particular topic or subject matter that addresses an important aspect of student development. How these choices are made about who will be assigned particular guidance activities varies from school to school, and each Advisory Committee can help establish the criteria for making these decisions.

An example in this section illustrates how counselors and advisory committees analyze needs assessments and summarize their findings into plans for a counseling program. It also shows that the school counseling program involves the services of many professionals in the school.

Marketing the Program

Counselors adopt a variety of methods to inform people about who they are and what they do in schools. These marketing strategies educate people about services available to students, parents, and teachers and promote the school counseling profession by counselors being visible in the schools and communities.

Samples of marketing and promotional strategies used by school counselors include:
• Brochures
• Counselor's Column in the school newspaper or local town newspaper.
• Web Sites about the counseling program and upcoming events and activities.
• Speaking Engagements at school meetings, civic groups, businesses, educational associations, and other organizations.
• Class Presentations to students about the counselor's role and services available.

Implementing

To provide a comprehensive program, school counselors must gain control of their time, and subsequently schedule services to satisfy the goals and objectives of the program as well as the critical needs of students, parents, and teachers.

Scheduling Services and Setting Priorities

As specialists who focus on broad areas of student development, school counselors have a unique role that distinguishes them from their teaching colleagues. One illustration of this difference is how counselors and teachers structure their time and establish their schedules.

In contrast to teachers' schedules, school counselors usually have more control over their daily routine. The schedule of a comprehensive school counseling program illustrates its attention to a wide range of preventive, developmental, and remedial issues.

School counselors seek suggestions from teachers and administrators in establishing their schedules so that their services complement rather than interfere with the instruction of students.

A counselor's schedule is also influenced by the goals and objectives selected after a needs assessment is complete. The process selected for setting priorities will influence the schedule of services.

By seeking suggestions from others, establishing schedules that fit the instructional program, and posting their schedules for others to see, school counselors accomplish several important goals. First, they demonstrate that the most important function of the school is to educate children and adolescents, and programs such as school counseling should enhance this process. Second, collaboration and cooperation with teachers place counselors in the visible role of letting people know what services are offered and when they are being implemented. Last, by seeking suggestions and establishing visible schedules, school counselors demonstrate that the services they offer are essential to the development of all students and are an integral part of the school.

Balancing Time

Nearly every resource that has been written to help school counselors establish comprehensive programs stresses the importance of time management. There is no mathematical formula or magic process that can help counselors balance their time across the varied services in their programs, but the different methods of setting priorities, presented in the previous section, provide a good starting point.

In addition to examining the priorities set by their Advisory Committees following the needs assessment, counselors can also identify the proportion of students who have critical needs. Typically, 10-20% of a student population is in need of some type of direct intervention. These students become the "focus group" of the counseling program, and should be given a high priority for individual and small group counseling services.

Once these "focus students" are identified and the counselor determines whether individual or group services are most appropriate, developmental needs of the remaining students should be addressed.

Figure 5.2 in the text illustrates a sample schedule of a middle school counselor. The sample schedule is an attempt to balance services for approximately 50 "focus students," and briefly shows how counselors might process the needs of a school to establish a reasonable schedule of services.

Counseling

Counseling in schools covers a wide range of issues and concerns, from peer relationships to suicidal thoughts. As such, counseling can address academic areas, personal adjustment, career decisions, and a host of other topics. Generally, school counselors offer short-term counseling relationships when dealing with serious and critical concerns.

Group counseling can help schools reach a larger number of students than can occur through individual counseling. In schools, group counseling is an essential service, yet it is often difficult to incorporate into the program due to scheduling problems, lack of suitable space, and misunderstanding about what it is.

Establishing Groups

When organizing and scheduling group counseling sessions and group guidance activities, school counselors develop a plan that informs the administration, educates the faculty, introduces groups to students, develops an acceptable schedule, and involves parents when possible.

Informing the Administration. Because group guidance and counseling services require special consideration to schedule students for sessions that remove them from normal class schedules and instruction, counselors should inform their principals about the nature and value of these activities. To convince their principals, school counselors readily demonstrate that group guidance and group counseling complement classroom instruction by helping students examine behaviors, attitudes, and perceptions that inhibit learning and restrict their development.

Persuading the Faculty. School counselors convince teachers of the importance of new services by demonstrating positive results in the services they already provide. Persuading teachers of the value and importance of group processes in a school counseling program is grounded in the assumption that students who work together learn essential skills and strengthen their self-perceptions.

Introducing Groups and Selecting Students

School counselors introduce their groups to students in a variety of ways. At the same time, counselors observe students during classroom guidance lessons and identify those who will benefit from either individual or group counseling.

Teachers, parents, and students are the referral sources who bring group ideas and suggestions to counselors.

When counselors select students to participate in small groups, they take precautions to assure compatibility of group members. In selecting students for small groups, school counselors consider age differences, language development, types of concerns, degree of concerns, and social class.

Selection processes are essential in creating successful groups. Corey (1990) surmised this screening process as an opportunity for the counselor to assess students and ascertain what they expect from the group. It is also an opportunity for students to become familiar with the counselor and the group counseling program.

By using a clear selection process, school counselors retain control over group membership. This is critical to their success as leaders of small group guidance and counseling.

Scheduling Groups

In designing group schedules, counselors determine the frequency of meetings, the length of each session, the place where they will hold sessions, and the number of sessions if they plan a closed group. Suggestions from teachers are essential in helping counselors design reasonable and efficient group schedules.

Scheduling large group guidance is not difficult if teachers and counselors integrate these lessons into daily instruction. As emphasized throughout this book, the most effective large group guidance occurs in the classroom as a result of a collaborative relationship between the teacher and counselor.

Small group guidance and small group counseling are more difficult to schedule, particularly if a counselor leads many groups involving a large number of students. To prevent students from missing the same subject matter every time their group meets, one solution is to stagger the times of the group meetings.

Involving Parents

Because group counseling and group guidance complement the instructional program of the school, counselors want to inform and involve parents in selecting children to participate in these services. In most instances, parental permission is not required for student participation in these programs, unless there is a local or state or other policy that stipulates the need for parental approval.

In some instances, students may want to join groups without their parents' knowledge. Whenever possible, counselors should honor and protect this request. For example, students who have been physically or sexually abused have the right to receive support and treatment without fear of retribution at home or elsewhere.

Consulting

School counselors assist parents and teachers with many aspects of child development and behavior. In most instances, counselors take the role of a consultant, bringing to the relationship a level of knowledge about human growth and development, needs of children and adolescents, and approaches for assisting students with behavioral changes.

Parent education programs and teacher in-service activities are forms of group consultation. Counselors also use consulting services when working with professionals outside the school. They frequently consult with health officials, social service workers, and professionals in other agencies to seek the most appropriate services for students and families.

Coordinating

Because a comprehensive school counseling program consists of several components and activities, it must be coordinated efficiently. Functions and skills that relate to program coordination include: scheduling services, providing clear communication, setting timelines, delegating responsibilities, following up services and commitments, and time management to name a few.

Appraising

To offer effective services, school counselors begin by gathering the necessary information to make appropriate and accurate decisions. When students are referred to counselors, a process of assessing the situation, appraising the student, and choosing appropriate services is required.

School counselors use many different appraisal methods including observations, interviews, review of records, tests, and inventories. When counselors fail to appraise situations fully and resort to using the same mode of operation regardless of the case at hand, they limit their power as collaborators and restrict the services of their programs. Counselors who perform adequate appraisal, make accurate diagnoses, and select appropriate services win the respect of their colleagues and the people who seek their assistance.

Evaluating

Accurate needs assessment, as seen earlier, is important to establish desirous school counseling services. By the same token, adequate evaluation is essential in determining the value of the services that counselors render. School counselors who design and follow through with reasonable evaluation processes are valuable members of their school staffs. Chapter 10 of this text describes evaluation procedures in detail,. This section serves as an introduction, and will highlight a few important elements of evaluation, particularly its practical considerations.

Evaluation in school counseling is an ongoing process of collecting data from students, parents, and teachers to assess services and activities. From a practical standpoint, an important consideration in designing evaluation processes is to keep it simple. School counselors do not have develop elaborate systems of evaluation that take time away from the very services they are attempting to deliver. That would be counter-productive.

Adequate evaluation enables the counselor and school to return to the assessed needs of students, parents, and teachers and the overall goals of the school counseling program. In this cyclical process, renewed planning, organizing, and implementing services continues.

Exercises

1. Design a brochure for an elementary, middle, or high school counseling program. Present the brochure to your class and ask them to critique it for clarity, brevity, and attractiveness.
   Rationale: Marketing strategies are important to successful programs. By having classmates critique students' brochures, you provide safe practice in this art.

2. Role play with another student and pretend that you are being interviewed on a radio program about being a counselor in a school.
   Rationale: Some marketing strategies will require live performances by students. Role plays offer a safe arena for practice.

3. Assess your time management behaviors. Make a list of the positive aspects of your time management, and then list the barriers to being a better time manager. How will you overcome these barriers when you are a school counselor?
   Rationale: Time management is essential for counselors. By examining the barriers they face to achieving better time management, students gain self-understanding that may help them in the future.

4. Visit a school counselor for a day and observe how that counselor organizes the program, implements services, and manages time.
   Rationale: Sometimes, observations can provide a great source of learning.

Test Questions

Multiple Choice Items

(b)   1. Planning, Organizing, Implementing, and Evaluating are
   (a) steps to diagnosing students' problems.
   (b) four phases of a comprehensive program.
   (c) four levels of evaluating school counselors.
   (d) aspects of marketing services.

(a)   2. A first step in designing a comprehensive program of services is to
   (a) examine the current program that is in place.
   (b) do research about school counseling services.
   (c) let teachers tell you what they want the counselor to do.
   (d) ask the principal what should be done first.

__(d)__   3. An Advisory Committee for a school counseling program
(a) is unnecessary if clear needs assessments are performed.
(b) must be appointed by the principal.
(c) always consists of parent volunteers.
(d) is a vehicle through which counselors obtain input about the program.

__(b)__   4. Needs assessments
(a) are usually cumbersome and unnecessary.
(b) are an essential part of program planning.
(c) should be performed only to evaluate existing services.
(d) should only be gathered on students.

__(a)__   5. Learning-related goals are selected
(a) to target specific learning objectives for students.
(b) by students and parents.
(c) to evaluate teacher performance.
(d) after service-related goals are selected.

__(c)__   6. "Hold one individual conference with each student during the year" is an example of
(a) a learning strategy.
(b) one way to mandate individual counseling.
(c) a service-related goal.
(d) limiting a counseling program.

__(b)__   7. A well-organized counseling program identifies goals and
(a) expects the counselor to provide all related services.
(b) assigns responsibility to those who will provide services.
(c) designates all instructional services to teachers.
(d) requires student participation.

__(d)__   8. Web sites, brochures, and speaking engagements are
(a) activities that counselors should avoid.
(b) information sources that detract from the counselor's normal duties.
(c) low tech to hi-tech strategies for providing counseling services.
(d) strategies for marketing counseling services.

<u>(a)</u>   9. In devising a schedule of services, school counselors
      (a) are wise to seek suggestions from their teaching
         colleagues.
      (b) should assert their professional autonomy as non-teaching
         personnel.
      (c) never see students when they are in classes.
      (d) should spend most of their time in classroom guidance.

<u>(b)</u>   10. Scheduling group services for students
      (a) is relatively easy in schools.
      (b) requires planning with teachers and administrators.
      (c) is the responsibility of the administrator.
      (d) is only necessary for classroom guidance.

Chapter 6

Individual Counseling and Group Procedures

OBJECTIVES

1) Define counseling, particularly as used in schools.
2) Illustrate how school counselors choose to use individual counseling in their programs of services.
3) Explore common approaches to counseling used by school counselors.
4) Distinguish the different group procedures used by school counselors.
5) Present a rationale for using group work in schools.
6) Examine the research regarding counseling and group procedures.

CHAPTER SUMMARY

This chapter presents counseling and group procedures as essential services in school counseling programs. It defines counseling, describes the school population who needs and benefits from counseling, discusses the goals of counseling, and illustrates the counseling process. In addition, this chapter suggests a role for brief counseling and crisis intervention in schools. Four approaches, compatible with school practice, are presented: Adlerian counseling, reality therapy, cognitive-behavioral approaches, and invitational counseling.

Although individual counseling relationships are effective in helping certain students, one-to-one processes are not always the most efficient use of a counselor's time and resources. The second part of this chapter focuses on two types of group processes used specifically with students: group counseling and group guidance. It describes the various group procedures used by school counselors, and explores the advantages and limitations of group counseling and group guidance. The chapter ends with a summary of research about counseling and group procedures.

Concepts and Events

- goals of counseling
- primary empathy
- advance empathic response
- "being with"
- unconditional positive regard
- congruence
- eclectic philosophy
- voluntary participation
- parental involvement

Names

- Carl Rogers
- Lopez (1985)
- Myrick (1993)
- de Shazer (1991)
- Alfred Adler
- William Glasser
- Albert Ellis
- Don Meichenbaum
- William W. Purkey
- Helen Driver
- George Gazda

Terms

- counseling
- closure
- Individual psychology
- Rational Emotive Therapy
- Invitational Counseling
- open group
- group counseling
- group consultation
- psychotherapy
- solution-focused counseling
- Reality therapy
- cognitive-behavioral approaches
- closed group
- group guidance

CHAPTER SYNOPSIS

What Is Counseling?

The counseling profession has discussed, presented, debated, and labored over this question since its beginning.

In addition to myriad theoretical orientations and varied views on process and content, the diverse locations and settings in which counselors practice compound the difficulty of arriving at a single precise definition of the counseling practice.

Counseling in schools is a process of helping students, parents, or teachers learn about themselves, understand how their personal characteristics, human potential, and behaviors influence their relationships with others, and make choices to solve current problems while planning strategies for optimal development.

Who Needs Counseling?

In deciding whether or not counseling is an appropriate service in a given situation, counselors investigate a number of criteria and ask several questions. Some of the questions counselors ask in reviewing criteria are:

1. Does the counselee see the situation in ways similar to those who made the referral?
2. Does the counselee perceive a need for assistance and accept counseling as a method of addressing this concern? Not all change.
3. How much control does a prospective counselee have in bringing about necessary change?
4. Is the counselee committed to making changes, learning new behaviors, or seeking alternatives to the present situation?

The answer to the question, "Who needs counseling?", depends on the goals and objectives of these helping relationships.

Goals of Counseling

The primary purpose of school counseling is to enhance educational planning, expand opportunities for learning, and strengthen students' achievement. This goal will be elaborated further in Chapter 9. School counselors should consider the following guidelines when selecting goals for individual counseling:

1. Relate goals to some aspect of learning.
2. Generalize the achievement of educational goals to other relationships.
3. Share learning experiences and skill development with others.
4. Involve parents whenever possible.

Individual Counseling in Schools

The following sections illustrate a four-stage approach to the counseling process.

Establishing a Relationship

Through the process of sharing feelings and perceptions, counselors and counselees establish beneficial interactions in the helping process and move from this introductory phase to a deeper and more meaningful exploration of concerns.

Exploring Concerns

Counselors guide their clients through adequate exploration of pertinent issues and toward selection of alternatives for resolving conflicts, gaining greater awareness, and making life-enriching decisions.

Taking Action

A relationship that fails to include definitive action to address a client's concerns is not counseling. The action phase of a counseling relationship enables clients and counselors to realize the goals they have chosen.

Ending the Relationship

All relationships come to an end, either naturally or circumstantially. Counseling relationships are no different. They too complete a final stage, which is called closure or termination. In school counseling, the process of ending or concluding a helping relationship deserves extra care and consideration. Because many interactions between students and counselors are ongoing, closure of an individual counseling relationship must be planned and done gradually.

Although no exact number of session can (or should) be assigned to counseling relationships in schools, contemporary approaches have encouraged models for brief counseling.

Brief Counseling

Brief counseling is particularly valuable in schools where time constraints are crucial to counselors. By way of summary, brief counseling usually centers on specific concerns or behaviors of students and tends to be an action-oriented approach. As examples, three separate, yet similar, models are given in the text [Lopez (1985), Myrick (1993), de Shazer (1991)].

Another application of brief counseling models is with crisis intervention. Schools reflect the trends and concerns found in society, and as a result, crises that occur in families and communities are often brought into the school house.

Crisis Counseling

Crisis situations require immediate intervention that includes assessment to determine the degree of risk and the level of crisis that students face. Crisis counseling, by nature, tends to be directive and action-oriented.

All forms of counseling, whether for brief therapy, crisis intervention or ongoing helping relationships, require a high level of leadership and facilitative skills to help clients reach their goals.

Counseling Approaches and Models

School counselors face the challenge of helping students, parents, and teachers evaluate their situations, explore concerns, examine alternatives, and make decisions within a reasonable period of time. This makes it palatable for school counselors to adopt an integrative posture, choosing from a range of approaches found to be successful in school settings.

Adlerian Counseling

The principles of Adlerian psychology adapt well to the practice of counseling in schools. In individual and group counseling students explore their positions in families, examine perceptions of self and others, confront detrimental actions, and establish goals for becoming responsible in personal and social lives.

Reality Therapy

The focus of reality therapy on personal responsibility and the power of the individual to make choices to gain control of life is appealing in school settings that emphasize learning and instruction. Its effectiveness has been suggested and documented in a number of areas including work with special student populations, student self-concept, and self-directed behavior.

In recent years, Glasser has taken his model of reality therapy and applied its principles toward the goal of creating "quality schools." Sometimes aligned with the "Total Quality School" movement, the "quality schools" approach dismisses traditional coercive styles of management and encourages cooperative and collaborative processes in much the same way that reality therapy involves clients in positive ways to take control of their lives.

Cognitive-Behavioral Counseling

Cognitive approaches, such as rational-emotive therapy and cognitive behavior modification, have been successful with school-age clients. In addition, these approaches have been used to teach self-counseling skills to students.

Invitational Counseling

This approach embraces a broad perspective of the services needed to help students, parents, and teachers meet the diverse challenges of today's world. At the same time, it encourages school counselors to move beyond the alleviation of immediate concerns towards the exploration of relatively boundless potential for future student development.

Invitational counseling is founded on the assumptions of perceptual psychology and self-concept theory. By considering the power of human perception and the impact of self-concept on human development, it advocates for school counseling programs that incorporate beneficial human relationships, improved physical environments, and respectful systems in which students can thrive.

The four approaches to counseling presented here offer a limited selection of theories of professional practice available to school counselors. Person-centered counseling, which evolved from the writings and research of Carl Rogers, offers school counselors a humanistic philosophy and foundation for basic helping skills that are essential for all effective counseling relationships. The four approaches highlighted here each relies on the therapeutic principles put forth in the person-centered approach.

Group Procedures

Although individual counseling relationships are effective in helping certain students, one-to-one processes are not always the most efficient use of a counselor's time and resources. Group methods allow counselors to reach out to more people and effectively use the helping potential of others.

A Rationale for Group Process

School counseling programs, in the context of group guidance and group counseling, provide the structure to help students learn empathic behaviors, problem-solving skills, and a host of cooperative, pro-social attributes. By advocating more group processes in the instructional and counseling programs of the school, counselors lend their expertise to the process of restructuring education and enhancing student development and learning.

Group Counseling and Group Guidance

Group counseling and group guidance are two processes used by school counselors to handle a wide range of students' concerns and interests.

Purpose and Nature of Groups

An essential difference between group counseling and group guidance is that counseling creates a confidential and personal relationship, and group guidance is more instructional and informational in nature. Additional differences between group counseling and group guidance are found in (1) the purposes of the groups, (2) the level of personal interactions among group members, (3) the leadership behaviors of the counselor, and (4) the size of the groups.

Size of Groups
Determining the size of groups depends on the purpose of the group, age of the group members, the number of sessions scheduled, and the nature and severity of problems mentioned by prospective group members.

Group Procedures and Comprehensive Programs
Literature indicates that some school counselors have become discouraged with implementing small groups because of resistance from teachers, administrators, or parents. At the same time, other counselors resist the use of group processes due to feelings of inadequacy regarding their leadership skills and abilities.

Group Structures

In small group guidance and group counseling, there are essentially two types of structures—open and closed. I recommend that school counselors choose closed groups because schools are often rigid organizations with precise schedules and traditional routines. Open groups may be confusing and difficult for students who have to remember which group they are in, and when their groups meet.

Each member's voluntary participation in a group, as opposed to involuntary assignment, can make a significant difference in how a group functions. Even though some students' assignment to particular groups may be involuntary, it is essential that their actual participation—sharing, self-disclosing, and supporting others—remain voluntary.

Leading Groups

Small group guidance involves communication skills similar to those used in counseling, and presentation skills used in classroom guidance.

In both group counseling and small group guidance it is important that counselors retain their leadership role. Combined with effective counseling skills, ground rules and other structural aspects of establishing groups increase the likelihood that group counseling and small group guidance sessions will be successful.

Advantages of Group Counseling

1. Group counseling offers a social setting in which students can share concerns, practice new behaviors, and support one another in a safe, nonthreatening environment.
2. By sharing their concerns in groups, students learn about and identify with common issues and perceptions held by others.
3. Group counseling encourages listening and facilitates learning.
4. Controlled "peer pressure" can be used in groups to encourage and confront students about their behaviors, goals, and attitudes that inhibit their development and progress in school.
5. Group counseling is action-oriented.
6. Group counseling can be less intense and threatening than individual counseling.
7. Group counseling is economically more efficient than individual counseling because more students can receive services in the same time span.

Limitations of Group Counseling

1. Effective group work takes a high degree of leadership skill. Group counseling is more complex than individual counseling because the factors to consider and the dynamics of the process are multiplied.
2. Group counseling requires a high energy level from the counselor to keep track of the group direction, address members equally, and establish effective relationships.
3. Scheduling groups, as noted earlier, can be difficult.
4. Group counseling may not be suitable or effective with some students.

Advantages of Group Guidance

1. In group guidance, counselors and teachers can impart information or instruction to larger numbers of students.
2. Group guidance does not require any special training in counseling theories and techniques since it uses instructional processes.
3. Guidance is best implemented as an interdisciplinary approach.
4. Group guidance has the potential to enhance the total environment of the classroom or school by emphasizing positive aspects of human development and relationships.

Limitations of Group Guidance

1. Because guidance groups are more educational and informational than they are therapeutic or personally enhancing, they may not result in significant changes with students who have critical conflicts or serious difficulties in their lives and in school.
2. Depending on the size of the group, guidance activities do not allow as much interaction among group members, as do group counseling sessions.
3. Group guidance does not necessarily offer consistent assistance toward specific personal, educational, or career goals for all group members.
4. Because group guidance uses instructional processes and techniques, and the size of groups is sometimes 25 or more students, counselors need to be more structured and directive in these activities.

Research on Counseling

Much of the research on counseling has focused on the "core conditions" first proposed by Carl Rogers. Research of other counseling models has indicated that these qualities are universally important to all helping relationships.

Presently, the research does not support any particular approach to counseling as being more effective than others. Research examining the effectiveness of counseling approaches and techniques confirms past findings and indicates that successful counseling relationships include mutually interactive processes in which counselors are empathic, involved, warm and credible in the eyes of their clients. The most crucial aspect of counseling . . . seems to be the skillfulness of the counselor implementing the intervention.

Numerous studies from the 1970s and 1980s have indicated that students who received counseling services showed improvement in attitudes, behaviors, and academic performance. Effective school counselors keep abreast of research findings about counseling and other services they provide.

Research on Groups

Research studies of group processes have increased in the counseling literature in recent years. Although research methodology has improved in recent years, some areas of group counseling need additional study, and some existing problems with research methods need to be corrected.

Group Guidance Research

This section summarizes several studies of groups that appear to be instructional or information in nature, and therefore are classified here as group guidance.

Group Counseling Research

Research on group counseling covers a broad area of treatment topics, student behaviors, and models of counseling. This section offers a few examples of studies using group counseling with student populations.

Exercises

1. Visit a school for a few hours during the day. Your goal during this visit is to observe the one-to-one interactions between students and teachers, students and students, and students and counselors. Note differences and similarities among these three pairs of interactions. Present your findings in class and discuss their implications. *Rationale: Part of learning one's own style of counseling is observing the process of helping as performed by others.*

2. In a small group, talk about the many one-to-one interactions a school counselor has with students, parents, and teachers during a typical day. List as many of these as your group can in a minute. Once your list is made, determine which of these interactions would be considered "counseling relationships." What factors did you use to identify those interactions that are counseling?

Rationale: Counselors perform a variety of functions and many of these consist of one-on-one relationships. It is helpful for students to identify the differences and similarities among these functions.

3. List five beliefs you now hold about human development. Specifically, think about: (1) why people choose the behaviors they do? (What causes behavior?), (2) what conditions affect a person's success in life?, and (3) how people can change After you have written your list of beliefs, share them with a classmate and decide what theory of counseling is most aligned with your assumptions. *Rationale: To develop one's personal theory and approach to counseling, a counselor must first learn about his or her beliefs regarding human development.*

4. Several research studies have found that group guidance can have positive effects on student variables. Review studies of group guidance effectiveness within the past ten years and note how many of them compared counselor led groups with teacher led groups. Summarize your findings for a class discussion. *Rationale: Knowing the research regarding the effectiveness of group procedures is the first step in persuading teachers and administrators of the efficacy of using these processes.*

5. In a small group think of topics that might *not* be appropriate for group counseling in a school setting. If there are such topics, how would you suggest school counselors address them if not through group processes? *Rationale: New counselors are sometimes confronted by community concerns about sensitive topics addressed in schools. This exercise allows students to explore their own perceptions of what is and is not appropriate for groups, and to search for alternative services.*

6. A new school counselor has confided her apprehension about doing large-group guidance with middle grade students. She was a mental-health counselor before coming to the school setting and has never worked with large groups of students. What recommendations would you give that would decrease her anxiety and build confidence in her ability to lead groups? *Rationale: All new counselors have some apprehension about doing groups because of their visibility. Having students explore their own recommendations to address this anxiety gives them a background to use when they become counselors.*

Test Questions

Multiple Choice Items

__(d)__   1. A first step counselors take in accepting a referral from
          teachers to counsel a student is to
   (a) test the student to check ability level.
   (b) place the student in group counseling.
   (c) begin individual counseling with the student.
   (d) observe the student in the classroom.

__(b)__   2. The differences between counseling and therapy
   (a) have been clearly delineated in literature and research.
   (b) are still debated among helping professionals.
   (c) are the same as between education and counseling.
   (d) are only important when considering school counseling.

__(b)__   3. Establishing a relationship, exploring concerns, taking
          action, and ending the relationship are
   (a) stages of student social development.
   (b) general phases of a counseling relationship.
   (c) developmental stages of a healthy personality.
   (d) a decision-making model for social intercourse.

__(c)__   4. Genuineness, empathy, positive regard, and concreteness
          are
   (a) self-concept traits essential for student development.
   (b) not as important as behavioral outcomes in counseling.
   (c) considered some of the "core conditions" of effective
       counseling.
   (d) not necessary when doing behavioral counseling.

__(b)__   5. Adlerian approaches to counseling believe that individuals
          are motivated by
   (a) instinctual desire.
   (b) social responsibility.
   (c) external reinforcement.
   (d) aversion and punishment.

__(d)__   6. Reality therapy is appealing to school counselors because it
   (a) relies on past events during the developmental years.
   (b) is relatively simple to use.
   (c) is manipulative in the techniques it uses.
   (d) focuses on personal responsibility and individual choice.

_(b)_   7. An advantage of cognitive-behavioral approaches to counseling is
(a) the short time in which change in behavior occurs.
(b) the emphasis on instructional methods.
(c) they rejects the notion of "self-talk."
(d) the reliance on effective punishment to bring about compliance.

_(d)_   8. Invitational counseling is founded on
(a) psychoanalytic theory.
(b) the Progressive Movement of John Dewey.
(c) models of behavioral therapy.
(d) self-concept theory and perceptual psychology.

_(b)_   9. One difference between group counseling and group guidance is that
(a) they focus on different age groups.
(b) group guidance activities can be presented to large audiences.
(c) leadership skills are not as important in group counseling.
(d) guidance groups are confidential.

_(c)_   10. Two types of group structures are
(a) limited groups and unlimited groups.
(b) classroom groups and small groups.
(c) open groups and closed groups.
(d) teacher-lead groups and student-lead groups.

_(c)_   11. One advantage of group counseling is that it
(a) can focus on serious pathological problems.
(b) is quick and efficient.
(c) uses controlled peer pressure to encourage students.
(d) does not require much training.

_(b)_   12. A limitation of group counseling is that it
(a) cannot be done when students have class.
(b) requires a high level of leadership skill and energy.
(c) is only useful with acting out students.
(d) requires parent permission.

_(c)_   13. Research on group guidance indicates that it
(a) is not effective in teaching appropriate behaviors.
(b) is more effective than group counseling in changing self-concept.
(c) can have a positive effect on students' attitudes.
(d) has little benefit for students in high school.

<ins>(c)</ins>   14. A difficulty of organizing group counseling in schools is
   (a) getting students who are interested in participating.
   (b) keeping the group topics secret.
   (c) setting a schedule for group sessions.
   (d) finding trained counselors.

<ins>(a)</ins>   15. While the research does not support any particular
        approach to counseling, there is some indication that a
        crucial aspect of successful counseling is the
   (a) skillfulness of the counselor.
   (b) major theory followed by the counselor.
   (c) age and experience of the counselor.
   (d) number of years the counselor has taught school.

Matching Items

COLUMN A		COLUMN B	
<ins>(e)</ins>	Albert Ellis	A.	internal dialogue
<ins>(j)</ins>	Alfred Adler	B.	set number of members
<ins>(g)</ins>	William Glasser	C.	group guidance
<ins>(f)</ins>	Helen Driver	D.	integrating approaches
<ins>(a)</ins>	Don Meichenbaum	E.	Rational Emotive
<ins>(h)</ins>	Carl Rogers		Therapy
<ins>(i)</ins>	S. de Shazer	F.	early author of group work
<ins>(d)</ins>	eclecticism	G.	reality therapy
<ins>(b)</ins>	closed group	H.	person-centered
<ins>(c)</ins>	instructional group		counseling
<ins>(k)</ins>	therapeutic group	I.	solution-focused
			counseling
		J.	Individual Psychology
		K.	group counseling

Chapter 7

Collaboration with School and Agency Professionals

OBJECTIVES

(1) Present the role of school counselors as collaborators with other professionals and agencies.
(2) Describe the different ways consultation is used by school counselors.
(3) Examine consulting roles.
(4) Review the research about consultation, particularly as used by school counselors.

CHAPTER SUMMARY

Although school counselors have primary responsibility for developing comprehensive programs, they cannot fully meet this challenge without assistance and support from other professionals in the school system and the community. For this reason, school counselors systematically initiate collegial relationships with a variety of educational, medical, and other professionals who provide auxiliary services to school populations.

In this chapter, students will learn about the many individuals, professionals, and agencies with whom school counselors create and maintain working relationships on behalf of students, parents, and teachers. In addition, this chapter presents an overview of the consulting skills and processes that enable counselors to establish and facilitate collaborative relationships with these different participants.

KEY CONCEPTS, EVENTS, NAMES, AND TERMS

Concepts and Events

- Parental involvement
- Educational for All Handicapped Children Act
- Child abuse and neglect
- Triangular structure
- Consulting modes

Names

- Verne Faust
- G. Caplan
- Dwayne Kurpius

Terms

- Least restrictive environment

School Services

Today's schools and school systems consist of a multitude of professionals and volunteers who provide countless services to students, parents, and teachers. In comprehensive programs, school counselors interact, directly and indirectly, with all these groups.

Parents and Guardians

The apparent trend toward longer parental involvement in children's developmental and decision-making processes has an effect on the overall involvement that parents expect to have in their children's education. By consulting with parents, school counselors design support networks and channels of communication to complement the goals and objectives of counseling with students.

When collaborating with parents and guardians, school counselors create many avenues through which they provide direct services or offer indirect assistance.

Teachers

Teachers are a vital link in the integration of affective education into the curriculum and they are the first-line helpers in the school counseling program.

Collaboration between counselors and teachers also occurs when they cooperate to plan and present in-service activities for staff development.

Teachers of Exceptional Children
Other teachers who are especially important collaborators with school counselors are the teachers of exceptional children.

Because school counselors provide services for all students in schools, they especially want to collaborate with special education teachers in assessing students' needs, locating school and community resources, planning counseling services, and examining school policies that have positive or negative effects on the educational progress of exceptional children and adolescents.

Principals

By establishing working relationships with their principals, school counselors are better informed about the parameters within which their programs of services need to function. Similarly, effective communication with administrators allows counselors the opportunity to convey their assessment of students' needs and the overall school climate, and how these two elements interact in the school.

Nurses, Psychologists, and Social Workers

Effective collaboration among these student services' professionals begins with a mutual understanding and respect for their unique roles in schools and regard for their individual areas of expertise. One form of collaboration is a team approach where student services staff members meet on a regular basis.

Community Agencies

Schools alone cannot offer all the human services necessary to help a town, city, or county educate its citizens, provide health care, and offer basic services to improve the human condition. When services offered by schools are insufficient to remedy the concerns of students and families, counselors and teachers turn to community resources.

Health Departments

School counselors rely on community health services to assist families with medical check-ups, tests, and offer recommendations to the school about health and medically related issues affecting the educational development of students.

Mental Health Centers

At times, the emotional and personal concerns of students require in-depth, intensive interventions. Time, schedules, and other factors associated with comprehensive school- based programs make it appropriate to refer these students and their families.

Social Services

School counselors and teachers are usually the first to learn about severe economic losses and limitations of families, and therefore, they are frequently in touch with departments of social services in their communities.

In addition to these severe economic needs, children and adolescents in many families are increasingly at physical and emotional risk due to neglect and abuse.

Family Services

It is impossible to separate students' concerns from their interactions with family members. For this reason, school counselors establish collaborative relationships with clinics and professionals who specialize in family counseling services.

In some instances, school counselors work with entire families. Models of family counseling for implementation in school counseling programs have been encouraged in the counseling literature.

In most comprehensive school counseling programs, family counseling and parent education services are limited. School counselors who provide family services continue to rely on community agencies and private practitioners as primary referral sources.

Private Practitioners

Physicians, counselors, clinical social workers, and psychologists in private practice offer an array of services to children, adolescents, and families to assist with educational, psychological, and social development. By identifying private practitioners in their communities, school counselors expand the list of resources available to students, parents, and teachers.

Counselors as Consultants

Research has shown that school counselors spend a considerable amount of time in consulting relationships.

The skills and processes associated with the different consulting roles assumed by school counselors are similar to other helping relationships they establish. Yet, structurally there are differences.

Consulting Processes

School counselors use consultation in a broad context that includes educational, informational, as well as problem-solving relationships. Consultations usually form a triadic relationship consisting of the counselor-consultant, a consultee, and a situation with a person (the client) or other external concern. Figure 7-1 in the text illustrates the triangular nature of most consultations used by school counselors.

Four generic modes of consultation have been presented in the literature. The *expert mode, prescriptive role*, *collaborator mode*, and *mediator mode.* To these four modes, I add *instructor* as a fifth consulting role for school counselors. This is usually the role school counselors take in parent education programs, teacher in-service, and classroom guidance with students.

The use of consulting processes in school counseling programs to convey information, offer instruction, or resolve difficult situations requires the application of different processes.

Informational and Instructional Consultation

The processes and skills used to convey information and present instruction are similar. Instructional approaches can be classified into four categories:

• *Information processing* is one type of instruction used by school counselors to disseminate educational and career materials to students and parents.

• *Social interaction* approaches encourage participants to interact with each other to learn about the topics addressed in the program.

• *Individualized consultations* provide information and instruction in brief contacts with students, parents, and teachers.

• *Behavior modification* strategies are helpful in either individual or group consultations. Behavioral approaches with individual students can be helpful in teaching a skill or learning to cope with particular situations, and can be used to instruct parents and teachers in management skills for home and school.

Each of these approaches relies on particular processes and skills on the part of the counselor-consultant:

• *Preparation.* Successful instruction and information-sharing require adequate preparation of materials and time.

• *Presentation.* In many respects, successful guidance, in-service, and other presentations by school counselors depend on skills similar to those used by effective teachers.

• *Feedback.* To create learning environments in which people accept information and attain skills, counselor-consultants seek ongoing feedback from participants.

• *Evaluation.* Counselors measure the effectiveness of their presentations by asking two questions:

1. Has the information or content of the activity been acquired by the participants?
2. Have the participants indicated their satisfaction with the presentation?

Problem-Solving Consultations

Problem-solving and situational consultations performed by school counselors can be illustrated by a generic four-stage model that can be adapted to different, divergent theoretical perspectives.

- *Introduction.*
- *Exploration.*
- *Implementation.*
- *Evaluation.*

Effective consultation, either for problem-solving, informational, or instructional purposes, requires a high degree of leadership and communication skill.

Skills used without proficiency are potentially damaging to relationships. Another caveat in using consulting skills relates to timing. Even the best of intentions will miss their mark when they are ill-timed. Successful consultants know *what* to do, and equally important, they know *when* to do it.

Research on Consulting

Research on consultation is plentiful, but methodological problems are prevalent, making it difficult to draw concise and accurate conclusions. For one thing, consultation lacks clear description and definition due to the variety of structures and models proposed in the literature and used by counselors in schools.

Generally, research indicates positive results with many types of consulting services and programs used by school counselors. However, more and better designed studies are needed. By way of example, a few studies are summarized in the text.

Exercises

1. Investigate available services in your community. Use the local telephone book and other resources to compile a list of services that could be used as referral sources for students in schools. Divide these services into categories such as "family services," "substance abuse services," and others to determine the range of services available.
   Rationale: As resource people, beginning counselors will benefit from establishing a process to compile local agencies

2. Form a group of four with other students in your class. Design a role-play situation where one student is the counselor-consultant, a second is a parent, and a third is the teacher. Make up a situation in which the parent expresses a concern about the child's progress in school. During the role-play, the fourth member of your group is an observer who will give feedback about the various roles and

skills observed.
Rationale: Consultation is a major function and role-play situations provide a safe environment in which to develop skills.

3. Contact school counselors in the community and ask what if any parent education programs are used in the school. Establish a list of the most prevalent programs used by elementary, middle, and high school counselors. Some programs used by counselors may be original designs, and you may want to ask counselor for a copy to share with your class.
Rationale: It is important for counselors to keep up with the latest materials used in parent education and other group consultation.

Test Questions

Multiple Choice Items

(a)   1. Consulting relationships for counselors in schools include problem-solving, informational, and
   (a) instructional situations,
   (b) therapeutic conditions,
   (c) profit-making arrangements,
   (d) administrative duties.

(c)   2. The skills used in counseling relationships are
   (a) identical to those used in teaching,
   (b) unique from any other helping relationship,
   (c) similar to skills needed in consulting,
   (d) all psychodynamically related.

(b)   3. School counselors may provide more direct services than usual
   (a) when teachers do not have the time.
   (b) in rural communities where there are few public or private agencies.
   (c) if teachers need counseling.
   (d) when the principal is out of the building.

(d)   4. A first step for school counselors to become a resource is to
   (a) make sure their counseling center is located near the administration's office.
   (b) identify teachers with whom they can share confidential information.
   (c) ask their principals for a computer.
   (d) learn about professional services provided by the school and school system.

<u>(a)</u> 5. Parent education programs
(a) can be developed by the counselor or can come from
     commercial products.
(b) should only be offered in the evening so they do not
     interfere with daytime services of the counselor.
(c) are the least important service of a school counseling
     program.
(d) are popular, yet ineffective services.

<u>(d)</u> 6. Counselors who are committed to serving all students
(a) have unrealistic goals.
(b) should spend more time using parent education programs.
(c) will probably suffer burn-out.
(d) form collaborative working relationships with special
     education teachers.

<u>(d)</u> 7. In exceptional children's programs, the "least restrictive
     environment" means
(a) placing no more the 10 students in the class.
(b) that exceptional students need to be placed in more
     permissive environments.
(c) that counselors should see these students more often.
(d) that, as much as possible, handicapped students must be
     instructed in classes with non-handicapped students.

<u>(b)</u> 8. When sharing information with principals, counselors
(a) must abide by the requests of the principal.
(b) are careful to follow ethical and legal guidelines.
(c) should always have a third party present.
(d) should be guarded and say as little as possible.

<u>(c)</u> 9. According to this text, classroom guidance is
(a) not an important service of a comprehensive counseling
     program.
(b) best done by the school counselor.
(c) a form of instructional consultation used by counselors.
(d) an outdated function of school counselors.

<u>(a)</u> 10. Preparation, presentation, feedback, and evaluation are
(a) processes and skills used in instructional and informational
     consultations.
(b) four steps to problem-solving.
(c) processes taught to parents for tutoring their children.
(d) behavioral techniques taught to students who have poor
     study habits.

Matching Items

COLUMN A		COLUMN B
_(d)_	least restrictive environment	A. child abuse
_(a)_	legal duty to report	B. consultant/consultee/ situation
_(e)_	Verne Faust	C. *Systematic Training for Effective Parenting*
_(b)_	triangular structure	D. mandate for serving exceptional children
_(c)_	Adlerian principles	E. emerging role of school counselor-consultant

Chapter 8

Student Appraisal

OBJECTIVES

(1) Review appraisal processes used by schools and school counselors to measure students' abilities, attributes, achievement, and interests.

(2) Describe common assessment instruments and other techniques used by school counselors.

(3) Explain the procedures used by counselors to select appropriate assessment instruments and other techniques to use in schools.

(4) Review the conditions for ensuring the proper use of standardized assessment instruments in schools.

CHAPTER SUMMARY

School counselors often coordinate school-wide testing programs, administer individual assessments to students, and interpret test data to parents, teachers, and professionals who provide services to students. As such, student appraisal functions, those procedures used to collect and interpret data about students' abilities, achievement, interests, attitudes, and behaviors, remain an essential part of the school counselor's role. This chapter reviews standardized tests, testing procedures, and nonstandardized methods used by counselors in the schools.

KEY CONCEPTS, NAMES AND TERMS

Concepts

- Test bias
- Reliability and validity
- Test scores
- Personality

Names

- *Mental Measurement Yearbook*
- *Tests in Print*
- *Dictionary of Occupational Titles*

Terms

- Appraisal
- Assessment
- Individual analysis
- Interpretation
- Measurement
- Diagnosis
- Standardization
- Norms
- Measures of central tendency

Names (con'd)
• *Standards for Educational and Psychological Testing*
• *Responsibilities of Users of Standardized Tests*

Terms (con'd)
• Specimen set
• Correlation coefficient
• Criterion- and norm-referenced tests
• Content, criterion-related, and construct validity
• Observation
• Anecdotal record
• Rating scale
• Frequency counting
• Interval recording and time sampling
• Sociogram

CHAPTER SYNOPSIS

Several terms describe the scope of assessment and appraisal procedures in counseling. By understanding these terms, school counselors enable themselves to take an appropriate role in student appraisal.

Appraisal
Assessment
Individual analysis
Interpretation
Measurement
Diagnosis

Standardized Testing

In the controversy surrounding student appraisal no single issue has raised more concern, fueled more heated debates, and caused more public uproar than the use of standardized tests. One major criticism of using tests in schools and other settings has been their limitation with culturally diverse populations and the possibility of test bias.

School counselors have responsibility for assisting their schools and school systems in the selection, administration, and utilization of tests and test results.

Standardization

A test is a standardized measure when administered and scored according to uniform procedures. Test standardization, therefore, requires uniform testing conditions every time a particular test is given. Another aspect of standardization that allows for the comparison of scores across test administrations, or among students who take a particular test, is the use of *norms*.

Norm-Referenced Tests
Tests that compare an individual student's performance to the performance of a group are norm-referenced tests. Norm-referenced tests are helpful in comparing students' performance and achievement with other students in their age or grade level, but they have limits when evaluating student knowledge or mastery of subject matter.

Criterion-Referenced Tests
These tests are designed to assess student performance in terms of specific standards or learning objectives. Typically, criterion-referenced test results are reported as the percentage of correct items in a particular knowledge or skill area.

The important issue for counselors, principals, and teachers is knowing why they should select a particular test and whether or not it is a reliable and valid measure of the trait being assessed.

Selection of Tests

Because school counselors are professionals trained in tests and measurement, they often help their schools with the selection of tests to use in testing programs. In addition, counselors select assessment instruments, including tests, to use in individual student appraisal.

Counselors use a variety of sources to learn about new tests and keep abreast of research on testing.

Identifying the Purpose of a Test
Why is a test needed? What is the school, teacher, student, or parent trying to find out? How will the results be used? Based on the research of existing tests, which ones appear to offer what we need? Knowing the intended use of the test and the type of score reports desired helps schools to initiate the screening and selection process.

Considering Administrative Conditions

Will the test be administered individually or to groups of students? Do budgetary restrictions preclude the selection of particular tests? How much time will be required to administer the test? Are there other conditions or materials required that will affect the selection of particular tests? All factors for administering the test correctly are carefully weighed before making a decision.

Acquiring Specimen Sets

When a school narrows its decision to a few possible choices, counselors order specimen sets of the tests from publishers.

Validity and Reliability

Test *validity* pertains to the degree to which an assessment instrument actually measures what it says it does. Three major types of test validity are content, criterion-related, and construct validity.

Reliability is the consistency of test results and outcomes from other assessment processes. Reliability refers to the results obtained with particular instruments rather than to the instruments themselves. A test that does *not* offer reliable results, cannot be valid, and a test that is valid yields, by definition, reliable results. At the same time, reliability is not a *sufficient* condition for test validity.

Usefulness

A third aspect to consider in test selection is the usefulness of the instruments being considered. In establishing criteria to evaluate test usefulness, counselors and teachers consider the following questions:

1. Will the time they devote to planning, administering, and interpreting the tests be well spent?
2. Will the test produce usable results to develop an appropriate curriculum, alter instruction to meet individual student's needs, or enable people to make important educational and career decisions?
3. Are the test results reported clearly so that all persons who read them will understand them?

Using Standardized Tests

Counselors and teachers who select appropriate tests and learn to use the results for the benefit of individual student development and improved instruction for all students want to ensure the proper use of standardized tests.

Test Security

Test information that is disclosed to students intentionally, or learned by students incidentally, jeopardizes the reliability and validity of the results.

Administration

Counselors and other test coordinators should take pains to help teachers who are administering these tests learn proper procedures and adhere to specific published directions.

The goal of adequate test coordination is to create a setting in which students achieve optimal results so that accurate decisions and appropriate educational plans take place.

Interpretation

School counselors are involved in the interpretation of test data with students, parents, and teachers, and they attempt to use test results with each of these groups to provide adequate instruction, proper placement, and assistance in educational and career decisions.

Counselors who coordinate testing programs in schools are responsible for assisting school administrators and teachers in using test reports properly.

Types of Assessment Instruments

Tests and other assessment instruments differ in characteristics and structure.

Achievement Tests

Achievement batteries, surveys of a range of subject areas and learning objectives, are perhaps the most popular form of testing in schools. They are efficient, cost-effective assessments that provide a broad overview of student performance. Counselors also use individual achievement tests in the student appraisal process. Individual achievement testing has increased as a result of special education services to handicapped students and the need to screen all students being considered for placement in these programs.

Aptitude Tests

A second common test administered to students in schools is the aptitude test. Aptitude tests are sometimes in the form of multiple batteries of aptitudes. Sometimes, school counselors use individual ability tests to obtain a quick estimate of verbal and nonverbal functioning.

Interest Inventories

Because student appraisal consists of more than testing, school counselors incorporate other types of standardized instruments into their assessment processes. Among these are interest inventories such as career questionnaires.

Personality Inventories and Tests

A number of instruments are available to assess students' characteristics and traits that may be termed "aspects of personalities." Of course, the concept and construct of *personality* are vaguely defined and rarely agreed on factors in the assessment field.

Basically there are two types of personality assessment: personality inventories and projective techniques. Two examples of personality inventories used by school counselors are the *Mooney Problem Checklist* and the *Myers-Briggs Type Indicator* (MBTI). A second type of personality assessment, the projective technique, is rarely, if ever, used by school counselors.

Other Assessment Techniques

School counselors use a variety of assessment procedures to gather data with which to make effective decisions in their counseling relationships with students, and to help teachers plan and implement appropriate instruction.

Observations

Because observations fit so naturally into the school setting and can be enhanced by the reports of parents, it is understandable why they are readily used and recommended as an assessment technique. At the same time, however, caution is needed. Observational techniques are limited due to the perceptual biases and resulting inaccuracies of the persons who are observing.

Observations of students in schools can be formal or informal. Some of the methods and instruments used by school counselors include anecdotal records, checklists, rating scales, direct measurement of products, frequency counting, and interval recording and time sampling.

Anecdotal Records
Observations that enable teachers, parents, and counselors to record descriptions of particular student behaviors during a given situation are methods of anecdotal reporting.

Rating Scales
When gathering observational data, counselors frequently find that a structured form, such as a rating scale, helps the observer—teacher, parent, or counselor—remain focused on the behaviors, characteristics, or traits being evaluated. Some commercially produced rating scales are available for use in schools.

Checklists
Observers' checklists are similar to rating scales with one difference being the type of judgment required from the observer. Checklists only ask the observer to mark *yes* or *no*, indicating whether he or she observed a trait.

Direct Measurement of Products
Students produce many items and products that are useful in the appraisal process. Examples of students' products, which teachers and counselors can evaluate include homework papers, art work, class projects, and journals. They can also evaluate school records such as attendance reports, health cards, test records, and grade reports.

Frequency Counting
Sometimes parents and teachers can add to the assessment of particular problematic behaviors by keeping a record of the frequency with which these behaviors occur. Methods of counting the behavior could include pencil and paper tally sheets, electronic or mechanical counters, and abacuses of some kind. Frequency counting is particularly useful with behaviors that are clearly defined.

Interval Recording and Time Sampling
When behaviors and attributes are not clearly defined and observable, interval recording and time sampling are appropriate

techniques for assessment. There are several different types of interval and time-sampling procedures. With most, the evaluator determines the length of the observation period and divides it into equal segments or intervals. An observer then records when the identified behavior occurs during the time period, counts the number of intervals where the behavior was observed, and computes the percentage of time the behavior occurred.

Interviews

In a comprehensive assessment of student developmental needs, interviews with students, parents, and teachers are essential. In addition, counselors interview former teachers, social workers, physicians, and other professionals who might add to the profiles being developed.

Sociometric Methods

Sociometric methods help teachers and counselors evaluate student relationships, identifying students who are most often chosen by their peers and the ones who are social isolates. Figure 8-7 in the text illustrates a sample sociogram for a fifth-grade class.

Child Study Conferences

An additional method used by counselors, particularly at the elementary and middle grades, is a child study conference, sometimes called a staffing. At these meetings, counselors, teachers, psychologists, social workers, nurses, and other professionals pool their knowledge and assessment results to make decisions about services to students and families.

Biographical and Self- Expression Techniques

Although self-report techniques tend to be suspect in terms of their reliability and validity, informal processes can assist counselors in gathering information and establishing rapport in the helping relationship.

Writing
Students with at least limited skills in writing can participate in the assessment process through essays about themselves, their families, friendships, and school. Another form of writing that students can share with counselors is in a journal.

Play and Drama

Elementary counselors frequently use play in establishing relationships with students who have limited language development; gathering students' views on school, family, and friends. Middle and high school students also participate in different types of play or drama, such as games, role-play, experiential exercises, and other activities, in counseling relationships.

Art Work

Art work is another form by which counselors gather information and establish communication with students. Using clay, paints, and other media with young students frees them to express themselves in ways not bound by language skills and ability. Older students benefit from art work as well, including photography and cartoons.

All the techniques and activities described in this chapter add to comprehensive student appraisal. An important caveat for school counselors is that no single assessment instrument, process, or result should be used when making program decisions or planning intervention strategies.

Exercises

1. In a small group, each of you disclose an experience you had in a test-taking situation. As your group discusses these events, consider what factors or conditions would have made the experience different for you. Ask a group member to record these comments to share with the class.
   Rationale: Empathy for students involved in testing may best be developed by remembering one's own experiences.

2. Review the sociogram in this chapter and identify students that you think would benefit from counseling services. What type of counseling do you think would be helpful to these students? How would you approach these students to offer services?
   Rationale: Using the diagram in this way offers the opportunity for practical insight and application.

3. With another student, visit a classroom in an elementary, middle, or high school and observe for an hour. Record your observations on a notepad using the margin to record time intervals. After your observation, compare notes with the other student and check the consistency of your observations.
   Rationale: Observational skills and techniques are invaluable tools

for school counselors, and are best learned by doing.

4. Design an assessment instrument to evaluate physical surroundings. Use the instrument to assess the building in which you hold class, and discuss your findings. How will this type of assessment fit with your role as a school counselor?
   Rationale: Many assessment strategies used by counselors will be developed by them, including observation forms, surveys and other instruments.

Test Questions

Multiple Choice Items

__(b)__ 1. Tests that report a student's relative standing in a sample population are referred to as
(a) criterion-referenced tests.
(b) norm-referenced tests.
(c) mastery tests.
(d) population driven tests.

__(d)__ 2. In testing, construct validity refers to
(a) how accurately a test is timed.
(b) inter-correlation with different forms of the same test.
(c) how accurately a test predicts success.
(d) how accurately a test measures the abstract, psychological characteristics it claims to assess.

__(d)__ 3. Classroom observations by school counselors
(a) interfere with instruction.
(b) should only be done with standardized observation instruments.
(c) rarely gather reliable data because students behave differently with the counselor in the room.
(d) can provide information to evaluate student learning and behavior.

__(a)__ 4. Reliability of test results is
(a) essential for a test to have validity.
(b) an illusive construct.
(c) not as important as internal consistency.
(d) not as important as external consistency.

(c)   5. The spread of students' scores across the group is measured
         by
         (a) the mean score.
         (a) a standard score.
         (c) the standard deviation.
         (d) a bi-modal distribution.

(a)   6. One procedure counselors use in selecting tests and
         inventories is to
         (a) order and examine specimen sets.
         (b) have teachers choose the tests they think are best.
         (c) buy the least expensive instruments to save money for
             more important instructional materials.
         (d) purchase instruments with the oldest copyright dates
             because they are "tried and true."

(b)   7. Standardized assessments
         (a) must be given by the teacher who teaches the students.
         (b) are always administered according to uniform procedures.
         (c) are less reliable than teacher-made tests.
         (d) are impossible to perform in schools.

(b)   8. Ensuring adequate and appropriate interpretation of test
         results to students, parents, and teachers is
         (a) the sole responsibility of the school psychologist.
         (b) an essential responsibility of the school's testing
             coordinator.
         (c) not as important as ensuring test security.
         (d) best performed in group procedures.

(c)   9. Projective techniques in student appraisal are
         (a) more reliable than self-assessment questionnaires.
         (b) more structured than standardized inventories.
         (c) rarely, if ever, used by school counselors.
         (d) easier to use than introspective techniques.

(b)   10. Sociograms
         (a) are fun activities for students, but useless as assessment
             tools.
         (b) help teachers and counselors assess student relationships.
         (c) are inappropriate to use in school settings.
         (d) should only be used by licensed psychologists.

Matching Items

COLUMN A

(f)   mean
(j)   percentile rank
(b)   median
(g)   diagnosis
(i)   stanine
(h)   reliability
(c)   aptitude tests
(d)   anecdotal records
(e)   frequency counting
(a)   sociogram

COLUMN B

A.   peer group assessment
B.   50 %ile rank
C.   ability assessment
D.   teacher's comments
E.   behavioral observation
F.   average score
G.   judgment about services to offer
H.   consistency in results
I.   type of standard score
J.   based on normal curve distribution

Chapter 9

Educational Planning and Career Development

OBJECTIVES

(1) Examine the primary purpose for having professional counselors practice in school settings.

(2) Explore the role of career development and career planning in comprehensive school counseling programs.

(3) Promote the attitude that educational success for all students is an fundamental goal of school counseling programs.

(4) Illustrate through a case presentation how all the essential services of a school counseling program are combined to assist students with their development and leaning.

CHAPTER SUMMARY

The essential services of a comprehensive school counseling program target two major goals that: (1) assist students with educational planning and success; and (2) encourage students to explore a wide range of options and make appropriate decisions to satisfy their career development. These two goals are complemented by two additional goals of assisting students with their personal and social development.

This chapter emphasizes the primary targets of educational planning and career development. In doing so, it focuses on the concepts of educational decisions, lifelong learning, advocacy for all students, and aspects of career development. The chapter concludes with a case study that illustrates how all the essential services, presented in this and the previous chapters, come together in a comprehensive effort to help students.

KEY CONCEPTS, NAMES, AND TERMS

Concepts	Names
• Self-knowledge	• Norman Gysbers
• Life roles	• Robert Gibson
• Life career planning	• Marianne Mitchell
• Student advocacy	• NOICC
• Lifelong learning	• SOICC
• Gender and cultural stereotyping	• SIGI-Plus

Terms	Names (con'd)
• Individualized Education Plan (IEP)	• GIS
	• DISCOVER II
	• C-Elect
	• *Occupational Outlook Handbook*
	• *Dictionary of Occupational Titles*

CHAPTER SYNOPSIS

Primary Purpose of School Counseling

The services described in this text come together in a comprehensive program, enabling all students to develop their fullest potential, achieve educational success, and select appropriate career goals. This perspective includes four areas of student growth and development adapted here from the work of Gysbers and Moore (1981):

Self-knowledge and interpersonal skills are achieved through counseling services that increase students' self-awareness and acceptance of others.

Life roles, settings, and events emphasize how various life roles are interconnected.

Life career planning is another essential aspect of the overall educational process.

Basic studies and occupational preparation encompass the fourth domain of life career development, which consists of all the learning objectives found in a school's curriculum.

The primary purpose for employing counselors in schools is to provide services and activities that enable all students to achieve academically, reach higher levels of functioning in basic skills, assess their strengths and weaknesses, and gather appropriate information about career development.

Educational Planning for All Students

All students, from the most advantaged and enthusiastic to the most underprivileged and disinterested, require individual and group services to encourage educational planning, learn decision-making skills, and set goals for lifelong learning and achievement. School counselors have an obligation to assist in developing and implementing activities that offer a meaningful educational focus for all students.

Student Advocacy

A major responsibility of all school counselors is to assist school administrators and teachers in designing and implementing policies, programs, and processes that equitably support the educational and career development of all students. There is no single service or activity by which counselors demonstrate their advocacy role.

Lifelong Learning

Education is not an isolated, individual process, aimed at accomplishing finite goals. Instead, it is a continuous endeavor beginning at birth and ending with death. It is lifelong pursuit with limitless goals and divergent purposes.

Education is not simply a means to an end; it is a fuel that ignites inspiration, desire, compassion, and a host of other human dimensions and emotions that enable us to live our lives fully. School counselors play a key role in this effort through the services of their comprehensive programs.

Career Planning and Decision-Making

The early focus of vocational guidance on the selection of an occupation has broadened considerably to include all aspects of career development. In addition, the interaction among educational planning, personal development, career choices, and successful living has become clearer.

Gibson and Mitchell (1990) highlighted several aspects of the changing nature of the world of work that have meaning for school counselors:
> *Career development is a process of many opportunities and probabilities*
> *Gender and cultural stereotyping in career selection is over*
> *Higher formal education will not necessarily equate to greater career satisfaction.*
> *The present will no longer predict the future*
> *Career development is an interactive process*

Student Awareness

The school counseling literature has used aspects of career development, such as awareness, exploration, and decision-making, to structure career activities and design a career focus for programs at the elementary, middle grades, and high school levels.

A number of computerized career assessment programs are available for school counselors to use in helping students acquire pertinent information and guiding students towards appropriate decision-making. As with most areas of computer technology and software development, the availability of career information systems is ever-changing. Preliminary research on the effectiveness of some systems is promising, but additional research is needed in this area.

Another avenue that school counselors and teachers use to enhance student awareness, particularly about career opportunities, is through special events during the school year.

Exploration

Career exploration begins at the elementary school level as an expansion of guidance activities in the classroom and as special events such as field trips to local points of interest. At the middle grades and high school levels, career exploration becomes more clearly defined and focused for students. At the high-school level, career exploration most likely occurs as a result of special events or individual and small group counseling.

Ideally, high school curricula, as in elementary and middle schools, should include classroom career guidance so teachers incorporate career aspects of their subject areas into daily instruction.

In individual and small group counseling, as well as classroom presentations, school counselors use computer-assisted programs to encourage career exploration. In addition, they use other media and resources to facilitate this learning process.

Decision Making

Children and adolescents at all levels of education must be guided in their educational planning, because it is through this developmental process that students increase their likelihood of making appropriate decisions and consequently, successful career choices. Simple steps can be designed to instruct students in decision-making skills, but the complexity of making decisions is revealed when individuals begin to use the steps learned and apply their own values and other unique qualities to the process.

The essential services and primary purpose of comprehensive school counseling programs require a range of counseling and consulting approaches, technical skills, philosophical beliefs, and professional characteristics that counselors bring to their helping relationships. The following case study offers a brief illustration of how these approaches, skills, and beliefs merge in an expanded view of a school counselor's role.

Case Study of Johnny

(The case of Johnny is on page 250-252 in the text. It describes interventions used by a counselor and teachers to intervene on behalf of a third grade boy who had gained a reputation as a "behavior problem.")

Case Study of Gertrude

(The case of Gertrude is on pages 252-254 in the text. It describes the various interventions used by the counselor and teachers to assist an 18 year old African-American student who was identified as educable mentally retarded, with a history of epileptic seizures, from a poor family, and lengthy record of inappropriate school performance.)

The above cases demonstrates the wide range of services that school counselors deliver to help students, parents, and teachers address a variety of issues. In this way, comprehensive services, orchestrated to focus on specific goals, resulted in successful outcomes.

Exercises

1. Think about your decision to study the counseling profession. List the factors or experiences that led you to this decision. Discuss with a classmate or in a small group these factors and compare and contrast differences and similarities.
   Rationale: By examining our own development and the experience that influenced us, we place ourselves in stronger position to help others.

2. Interview a worker in any profession or line of work. Through your questions, discover how the individual came to choose his or her career track. Assess the person's satisfaction with the choice and ask what, if anything, he or she would change about that career choice, if anything. In class discussions, compare findings of these interviews.
   Rationale: Increasing one's knowledge about how people make career decisions and the relationship between those decisions and career satisfaction can be translated into future counseling relationships.

3. In a small group, list career changes that have been brought about by technological advances in the past ten years. After making this list, have your group predict which of these changes will be significantly altered again in the next ten years.
Rationale: Successful counselors always look ahead in helping their clients plan for the future.

4. Review the case studies of Johnny and Gertrude. In a small group, discuss the way each counselor approached the case. What challenges were faced, risks taken, and decisions made that played a significant role in each situation?
Rationale: By examining and discussing each case, students have an opportunity to explore their own thoughts about the risks they would have taken and the interventions they would have chosen.

Test Questions

Multiple Choice Items

(b) 1. A primary goal of school counseling programs is to
(a) encourage students to behave the way teachers want them to act.
(b) assist students with educational planning and career decisions.
(c) help students resist the rigid policies of educational institutions.
(d) demonstrate for parents appropriate ways to help their children learn.

(c) 2. A major challenge for schools is to
(a) indoctrinate students about particular career choices.
(b) help all students assimilate cultural mores.
(c) connect learning objectives with broader career goals of students.
(d) discourage parents from becoming too active in career planning with the children.

(a) 3. School counselors have responsibility to help their schools
(a) create curricula that meet the needs of all students.
(b) teach all the guidance classes in the curriculum.
(c) provide teachers with breaks from classroom instruction.
(d) keep students in ability groups.

_(c)_   4. By helping schools design equitable programs and
            procedures, counselors demonstrate
         (a) their administrative skills.
         (b) a superior knowledge of curricula issues.
         (c) advocacy for students.
         (d) an awareness of school and community politics.

_(d)_   5. The notion of "lifelong learning"
         (a) is beyond the scope of the school's responsibility.
         (b) should not be allowed to interfere with the school's daily
            routine.
         (c) has little value in educational planning.
         (d) should be fostered by counselors in their educational and
            career objectives.

_(a)_   6. Effective schools' research demonstrates that
         (a) parental involvement is related to quality education.
         (b) students learn best when grouped by their ability.
         (c) students' intelligence is more important than parental
            involvement in schools.
         (d) parents' level of education is more important than their
            participation in their children's education.

_(b)_   7. Future school counselors can expect that gender and cultural
            stereotyping will
         (a) continue to be major factors to consider in career
            planning.
         (b) gradually become less important factors to consider.
         (c) emerge in school texts.
         (d) become more acceptable in public schools.

_(c)_   8. Some evidence suggests that higher formal education
         (a) is absolutely related to personal satisfaction.
         (b) will no longer be recommended for the majority of
            students in the 21st Century.
         (c) may not necessarily equate to career satisfaction.
         (d) will be obsolete in the future.

_(b)_   9. In using computer-assisted career information systems,
            school counselors
         (a) should adopt only commercially produced programs.
         (b) stay informed about these ever-changing systems.
         (c) are reluctant to use commercial programs.
         (d) should use only programs produced by the National
            Occupational Information Coordinating Committee
            (NOICC) and its state divisions.

105

<u>(d)</u>   10. An essential part of helping students with their educational and career plans is

(a) to encourage them to select a career before high school.

(b) the parents' rights to know what their children share with school counselors.

(c) the school's responsibility to help the community fill its manpower needs.

(d) to teach them decision-making skills and processes.

Matching Items

COLUMN A		COLUMN B	
<u>(e)</u>	IEP	A.	national career information
<u>(d)</u>	stereotyping	B.	interactive career assessment
<u>(a)</u>	NOICC	C.	dictionary of career titles
<u>(b)</u>	SIGI-Plus	D.	"men only" careers
<u>(c)</u>	DOT	E.	planning process for exceptional students

Chapter 10

Evaluation of a School Counseling Program

OBJECTIVES

1) Learn why program evaluation is important to comprehensive school counseling programs.

2) Examine the role of the counselor, teachers, and principal in program evaluation.

3) Describe aspects and procedures of performance appraisal for school counselors.

CHAPTER SUMMARY

Beginning in the 1960s and continuing to the present day, the issue of accountability emerged as a requisite to the role and function of school counselors. Specifically, attempts to define and describe the role of school counselors has included an urgency to demonstrate effective practices.

School counselors as a group are reluctant participants in this movement towards accountability. Such avoidance of professional accountability continues as a major barrier to public recognition and acceptance of school counselors as essential contributors to effective educational programs.

This chapter examines two aspects of counselor accountability—program evaluation and counselor effectiveness. The purpose behind training counselors in these evaluation processes is three-fold: (1) to help counselors gather data with which to plan their own professional development; (2) to enable counselors to make a case of their value and worth for the decision-makers who plan school programs and services; and (3) to invite counselors to participate in research efforts that lend credibility and validity to accepted practices and the future development of their profession.

Concepts and Events

- Sputnik I, 1957
- *Nation at Risk*, 1983
- Accountability
- Goal Attainment
- Consumer satisfaction
- Counselor intentionality

Names

- *Professional Development Guidelines* (ASCA)

Terms

- Process evaluation
- Outcome evaluation
- External evaluation
- Performance appraisal

CHAPTER SYNOPSIS

Models and methods of accountability presented in the counseling literature suggest the following principles and guidelines:

1. The goals of a school counseling program must be defined and agreed on by all who will participate in the evaluation process.
2. All people who participate in, or are served by, the school counseling program should be involved in the evaluation process.
3. The instruments and processes used for gathering evaluation data should be valid measures of services and goals of the school counseling program.
4. Program evaluation is a continuous process aimed at identifying beneficial services and effective methods of service delivery.
5. Evaluation of school counselors must, by definition, enable supervisors and principals to demonstrate that the services provided in a comprehensive counseling program contribute to the school's ability to educate all students.
6. Equally important to helping the school reach its goals is the related purpose of enhancing the counselor's professional development and encouraging skillful improvement.
7. Both program evaluation and counselors' performance appraisal imply that action will be taken as a result of the findings gathered in the assessment process.
8. Evaluations are most helpful and effective when they emphasize positive goals.

Types of Program Evaluation

Program evaluation is generally of two kinds: process evaluation and outcome evaluation. Accordingly, *process evaluation* indicates whether the services and strategies planned for the program were carried out, and answers questions such as: How many people were served? How much time was spent on service delivery? How many sessions were held? *Outcome evaluation* is an assessment of the outcomes of the services that counselors provide in comprehensive programs.

The following sections review four methods of program evaluation.

Goal Attainment

The ultimate purpose of a school counseling program is found in its goals and objectives. Some goals are set as a result of local and state mandates and standards that aim at providing equal services to all students. In evaluating their programs, counselors measure goal attainment in two ways—through learning-related goals and service-related goals.

Learning-related Goals
Evaluating this type of goal requires the development of assessment instruments and processes to measure particular learning that is expected of the population being served.

Service-related Goals
By choosing a service-related goal, the counselor addresses the relationship between learning goals and services provided by the program. Reports that enable counselors and supervisors to examine where time is being spent and how many students, parents, and teachers are being served are important for program evaluation. However, these types of reports do not adequately address the effectiveness of services.

Student Outcomes

In all cases, the services counselors provide to reach specific goals should produce some measurable or observable result. Student outcomes can take several different forms. For example, evaluation can be based on predetermined or prearranged standards. Another type of outcome procedure compares students in a specific program with ones who have not yet participated. A third type of outcome procedure asks students to respond to their reactions and involvement in a particular service, or asks parents and teachers to observe and record their findings regarding changes in students' behavior and learning. A fourth type of outcome assessment uses a pretest and a posttest comparison.

Consumer Satisfaction

Some outcome research is essential to demonstrate the efficacy of counseling services, but if this is all counselors did, they would have little time to deliver the very services they were attempting to evaluate.

School counselors use different methods of gathering data from students, parents, and teachers to assess the overall level of satisfaction with program services.

By gathering data from the consumers of school counseling services, counselors and their supervisors are in a stronger position to make purposeful and meaningful decisions about future directions for the program.

Expert Assessment

Perceptions of local supervisors, including school principals, and from students, parents, and teachers offer counselors an opportunity to broaden their assessment of what services are effective and what new services may be needed. However, if only these types of internal perspectives are used, counselors and their supervisors will limit annual evaluations to restricted and repetitious views of *what should be*. To guard against this kind of parochial stance, counselors and supervisors occasionally seek assistance from outside experts in school counseling who offer an external perspective to the evaluation process.

By using outside experts to gather information, counselors and supervisors increase the objectivity of the evaluation process and thereby ensure more reliable results.

School Counselor Evaluation

On the whole, adequate evaluation of school counselors has been a rare occurrence. In recent years, there has been some indication that evaluation of school counselors is receiving more serious attention. Some states and local school systems have developed specific criteria and designed processes that are particularly suited for school counseling practice.

What Will Be Evaluated?

The first step in developing appropriate evaluation procedures for school counselors is determining their essential functions and identifying specific activities that define these functions.

How Will Evaluation Be Done?

Unlike teacher evaluation, which depends heavily on classroom observations, school counselor appraisal relies on diverse methods of data collection and documentation. Included in these methods are observations, interviews, simulated activities, self-assessments, product development, video and audio tapes, schedules, consumer feedback, records of services, and memos of personnel action.

Observations
Although some counseling services cannot be observed directly due to their confidential nature, other activities used by school counselors can be evaluated through observation.

Audio and Video Taping
When an observation would be an intrusion to the helping relationship, other methods of evaluation are recommended. An alternative method of collecting information is through the use of video or audio taping.

Interviews
Another method of gathering information about a counselor's performance is to interview the counselor about program plans, specific services, and student outcomes. The most effective use of interviews is with a structured format to focus on specific issues, skills, or other aspects of the school counseling program.

Simulations
When observations are inappropriate and taping is impractical, counselors and supervisors may find that simulated sessions are adequate for gathering information.

Self-Assessments
An evaluation is incomplete without the counselor's perspective. On way to include the counselor's perspective is to begin with a self-assessment. Self-assessment processes enable counselors to identify their own strengths and weaknesses and recognize these aspects of their professional practice.

Products
School counselors create many products and reports for their schools and programs. These items can be assessed as part of the overall performance appraisal process. Specific competencies that might be addressed by examining materials and reports produced by school counselors include: writing, program planning, and public

relations.

Consumer Feedback

Asking students, parents, and teachers for feedback in evaluating specific functions and activities is important in the overall evaluation of the school counseling program. These observations are also valuable in helping counselors assess their performance.

Schedules and Records

Part of an evaluation should include the plans that counselors write, the goals they set, the schedules they make, and the records they keep. Of all these evidences, records are ones that may be most difficult to include in the performance appraisal process. In all cases when counselors share these types of records, the client's identification must be deleted and the anonymity of the client maintained.

Personnel Memos

Finally, other documents to include in performance appraisal are memoranda used to cite specific instances where a counselor has not met a performance standard. Memos of visits, conferences, and plans of action, as well as other documents filed during this phase of the performance appraisal process, are essential in protecting the rights of the individual counselor, ensuring the integrity of the school counseling program, and verifying support offered by the supervisor and school system to remedy the situation.

Who Will Evaluate?

The last question to consider in designing a performance appraisal process for school counselors is, who will do the evaluation? In most instances, school counselors report directly to building principals who are ultimately responsible for the counselor's evaluation. The challenge is to find ways that counselors can receive appropriate supervision and accurate evaluation for the services they provide in schools.

One way to create appropriate performance appraisal procedures is for principals and counseling supervisors to cooperatively participate in the evaluation of school counselors. In many school systems, the luxury of having a trained supervisor of counselors is unrealistic due to fiscal constraints. In such cases, other models of supervision should be explored.

Performance Appraisal Processes and Instruments

School counselors not only assist in the development of appropriate procedures for their performance appraisal, they also participate in designing adequate tools with which to do an accurate assessment. Instruments designed to evaluate counseling services must be related to specific approaches and behaviors that are generally accepted as indicators of a particular professional practice.

Exercises

1. In small group, discuss a time when you were evaluated for your performance. Share your feelings about this experience, and talk about aspects of the evaluation that could have been changed to make it a more positive event. What aspects did you control that could have been adjusted to make the evaluation more helpful? *Rationale: It is important to explore one's feelings about evaluation and use this knowledge to gain self-control and self-responsibility in the evaluation process.*

2. Pretend you are a school counselor. Your principal has indicated that he or she wants you to document the effectiveness of your counseling relationships. What would you do in planning such documentation? Create the documents you would use and share them in class. *Rationale: Planning evaluation documents and processes prepares students for future experiences with principals, supervisors and other evaluators.*

3. Visit and interview a school counselor about evaluation methods he or she uses in assessing program effectiveness. If the counselor has any forms to share, bring them back to class and compare them with other forms your classmates obtain in their visits. Use these visits to stimulate discussion about what counselors are, or are not, doing to be accountable in their schools. *Rationale: It is helpful to take knowledge learned in course work and test it out in real experiences.*

4. As a way of comparing what counselors in non-school settings do for accountability, visit a counselor in an agency or higher education setting and ask the same questions you used for exercise 3 above. *Rationale: Since school counselors belong to the larger counseling profession, it may be helpful to see how other professional counselors plan and perform program evaluation .*

Test Questions

Multiple Choice Items

(b)   1. By using monthly report forms that indicate how many students received counseling, how many consultations with parents were held, and how many group sessions were presented, school counselors
(a) demonstrate that their services are more important than school psychology and other student services.
(b) are able to quantify how they spend their time.
(c) illustrate the quality of their services.
(d) demonstrate teacher satisfaction with the counseling program.

(c)   2. A major barrier to public recognition and acceptance of school counseling as a profession is
(a) lack of training for school counselors.
(b) school administrators' disrespect for counselors.
(c) school counselors' avoidance of program evaluation and professional accountability.
(d) teachers who undermine the school counselor's role.

(a)   3. Program assessment that attempts to measure the results of counseling services is
(a) called *outcome evaluation*.
(b) futile because counseling effectiveness cannot be measured.
(c) usually not a productive use of counselor's time.
(d) is the only true way to do program evaluation.

(d)   4. A "control group" research format attempts to demonstrate
(a) the democratic leadership style of the school counselor.
(b) group management skills of a counselor.
(c) the focus of a particular group session.
(d) a possible causal factor in bringing about a desired student outcome.

(a)   5. Survey instruments that assess the satisfaction of students, parents, and teachers with a school counseling program are
(a) examples of perceptual measures.
(b) a waste of time.
(c) norm-referenced evaluation instruments.
(d) too cumbersome for most school counselors to use beneficially.

(b)   6. School counselor evaluation is different from teacher
        evaluation because
        (a) nothing counselors do can be adequately observed.
        (b) there are so many possible methods of data collection.
        (c) we are not sure exactly what counselors are supposed
            to do.
        (d) it is difficult to measure counselor effectiveness.

(c)   7. When addressing the issue of counselor evaluation, a critical
        question for the school counseling profession is:
        (a) What benefit will students realize?
        (b) How do we determine what students should learn?
        (c) Who will evaluate counselors?
        (d) How much time will be needed for evaluation?

(a)   8. External evaluations of school counseling programs
        (a) can complement internal evaluations and avoid parochial
            perspectives.
        (b) are best be performed by counseling psychologists.
        (c) should only be done with the counselors' approval.
        (d) are the only way to arrive at clear results.

(b)   9. School counselor performance appraisal
        (a) should only be completed by school principals.
        (b) includes many different methods of data collection.
        (c) uses the same procedures and methods as teacher
            evaluation.
        (d) has had uniform practices established for many years.

(a)   10. School counselors should create methods of accountability
        in their programs
        (a) to demonstrate the value of their services and professional
            credibility.
        (b) because politics demand it.
        (c) so other people do not try to tell them what to do.
        (d) because it is part of a national movement to make schools
            more effective.

Matching Items

COLUMN A		COLUMN B
(d)	intentionality	A. perceptual data
(c)	process evaluation	B. avoiding a parochial perspective
(a)	consumer satisfaction	C. How many sessions?
(b)	external review	D. having purpose and direction
(e)	simulations	E. one method of assessing performance

Chapter 11

Professional Ethics and Legal Issues

OBJECTIVES

*(1) Introduce the Ethical Standards of the American School
        Counselor Association*
(2) Present legal aspects of education and schools
(3) Present legal issues common to school counseling practice

CHAPTER SUMMARY

School counselors practice according to standards, regulations,
laws, and codes that have been established by professional associations,
state and federal governmental bodies, the courts, and other institutions.
The ethical guidelines followed by most school counselors are the
Ethical Standards for School Counselors adopted by the American
School Counselor Association (see Appendix A) and the Ethical
Standards of the American Counseling Association.

Today's ethical issues are complicated by ever-changing social
structures and a technologically advancing society. So, while broad
topics are similar to those of years past, contemporary school
counselors experience increasingly complex issues when dealing with
ethical and legal questions.

This chapter presents the ethical standards developed by the
American School Counselor Association and considers legal issues
related to the ethical practice of school counseling.

KEY CONCEPTS, EVENTS, NAMES, AND TERMS

Concepts and Events

- Confidentiality
- Parents' rights
- Students' rights
- Professional responsibility
- Common law
- Case law
- Legal jurisdiction
- Family Educational Rights and
    Privacy Act of 1974
- Due process

Names

- *Ethical Standards for
    School Counselors*
- *Ethical Standards of the
    American Counseling*
    Association
- 14th Amendment
- 4th Amendment
- Buckley Amendment
- Public Law 94-142
- Title IX

- Privileged communication
- writ of certiorari
- Liability
- Malpractice

CHAPTER SYNOPSIS

Ethical Standards of School Counselors

The standards for school counselors are themselves not absolute guides for every decision counselors must make in their daily practice. Instead, they are general guidelines that enable counselors to establish a foundation of ethical behavior.

The ethical standards put forth by ASCA are divided according to the counselor's responsibilities with students, parents, and other professionals, the school, the counseling profession, and oneself.

Responsibilities to Students

School counselors have primary responsibility for ensuring that their counseling services and the educational program of the school consider the total development of every student, including educational, vocational, personal, and social development. The ethical guidelines state that school counselors should avoid imposing their values on counselees, and, as such, should encourage students to explore their own values and beliefs in making decisions about educational plans and life goals.

The ethical standards stipulate that school counselors will protect the confidentiality of students' records and information received from students in counseling relationships. Legally, the courts have not always recognized that minors have the capacity to understand and establish confidential helping relationships.

The term *confidentiality* refers to an individual's right to privacy that is inherent in professional counseling relationships. By contrast, *privileged communication* is a legal term used to indicate that a person is protected from having confidential information revealed in a public hearing or court of law.

In 1987, only 20 of the United States granted some form of privileged communication rights to students in school counseling relationship. When students share information indicating their intentions to harm themselves or others, or when they, themselves, are being abused, counselors cannot keep this information confidential.

Responsibilities to Parents

Counselors sometimes form helping relationships with parents in either counseling or consulting roles. Most if not all of the guidelines in Section A, Responsibilities to Students, of the ASCA ethical standards can be adapted to these helping relationships. Informing parents of the purposes and procedures to be followed and maintaining confidences are practices that apply to helping relationships established with parents as well as with students.

Section B of the ASCA standards pertains specifically to counselors' responsibilities for informing parents about services available to students, and involving parents when appropriate. Although the ethical responsibility for maintaining confidentiality between a counselor and student may be understood, the legal responsibility of counselors to involve parents in their helping relationships is not as clear.

Responsibilities to parents include the practice of providing accurate and objective information. Accordingly, counselors are obliged to share information about services in the school and community accurately and fairly without bias or discrimination.

Responsibilities to Colleagues and Professional Associates

A successful and effective school counseling program does not exist without cooperative relationships between and among teachers, administrators, and counselors. In addition, other educational specialists also cooperate with school counselors. These include school nurses, social workers, psychologists, and special education teachers. Implied in this section of the ethical standards is the counselor's responsibility to be informed about the effectiveness of these additional sources of information and assistance.

Ethical counselors keep lines of communication open, and within the limits set by confidentiality and privileged communication guidelines, they share and receive information to assess services that have been provided.

Responsibilities to the School and Community

Part of being a spokesperson for the welfare of students is accepting the role as an advocate for the educational mission of the school.

This section of the school counselor's ethical standards addresses the importance of defining and describing the counselor's role and functions in the school, and performing systematic evaluation of these services. School counselors should notify principals and supervisors when conditions in the school "limit or curtail their effectiveness in providing services" (American School Counselor Association, 1992, p. 15).

School counselors establish relationships with other professionals and agencies for the benefit of students, parents, and teachers without regard for their own interests.

Responsibilities to Self

The school counselor's ethical guidelines address the need for counselors to behave within the boundary of their professional competencies and accept responsibility for the outcomes of their services. A common dilemma for school counselors, which is related to this section of the standards, is deciding when to stop seeing a student in a counseling relationship and refer the student to another professional or agency.

Responsibilities to the Profession

School counselors who are members of the American School Counselor Association and follow the ASCA standards accept responsibility for behaving in an exemplary fashion on behalf of their colleagues and the profession they represent. These exemplary behaviors include the research that counselors perform, their participation in professional associations, their adherence to local, state, and federal regulations, and the distinction they make between privately held views and views they espouse as school counseling representatives.

Maintenance of Standards

School counselors are responsible for seeing that the ethical standards are followed, not only by themselves but by their professional colleagues, their supervisors, and the institutions that hire them.

When a counselor observes a violation of ethical standards, the guidelines encourage the use of available avenues within the school and school system to bring this problem to the attention of appropriate persons. If attempts to resolve the situation go unheeded or are rejected, the counselor's next step is to refer to an appropriate ethics committee in a school counselor association; first at the local level, then at the state level, and finally, at the national association level.

While ethical standards are the guidelines for appropriate practice established professional organizations, legal parameters are the policies and regulations set by governing agencies, statutes passed by legislatures, and ruling in courts of law.

The Nature of Law

The sources of laws in our society include: federal and state constitutions, statutes, case law, and common law. In addition, local school board policies and regulations, which must conform to state and federal laws, may also apply to the practice of school counseling.

The Law and Schools

When considering a particular legal issue involving education, counselors review pertinent court cases, local school board policies, state and federal laws, government regulations, and constitutional questions.

An initial source of legal information and understanding is the Constitution of the United States. Though no mention of education or counseling is found in this historic document, clearly as the "supreme law of the land" this document supersedes all other local and state regulations. Other sources of information that help counselors learn about the law are state statutes, local policy manuals, and legal briefs.

School counselors must be fully aware of local policies and regulations, especially those that apply to counseling and other student services in the schools.

The Courts

The legal system in the United States consists of federal and state courts. Federal courts hear only those cases pertaining to constitutional questions, such as equal protection under the law as granted by the Fourteenth Amendment of the Constitution. By contrast, state courts have broader responsibility for trying criminal and civil cases as well as those pertaining to federal and state constitutional issues.

State Courts

The fifty state court systems typically consist of four levels or categories of jurisdiction: district (or circuit) courts, courts of special jurisdiction, small claim courts, and appellate courts.

Federal Courts

The federal court system of the United States consists of nearly 100 District Courts, Special Federal Courts, 13 Courts of Appeals, and the Supreme Court. Eleven of the 13 Courts of Appeals rule in the judicial circuit of the United States and its territories.

When cases are appealed, they move from the trial courts that make up the U.S. District Court System to the Court of Appeals in the respective judicial circuit, and then to the Supreme Court. In addition, a case in the state judicial system can move from the highest state court to the U.S. Supreme Court in the form of a *writ of certiorari*.

School Board Policies

School districts have broad responsibility for developing and implementing regulations affecting schools within the limitations and guidelines set by state statutes. At no time does an individual school or school system have authority to legislate beyond the limits defined by the state.

Legal Issues for School Counselors

Because court rulings frequently change current thinking and existing policies regarding these issues, counselors need access to accurate, up-to-date information.

Student's Rights

There are many aspects of students' rights related to schooling, and some common issues include freedom of expression, the right to due process, appropriate/compensatory education, and the right to privacy.

The *Family Educational Rights and Privacy Act* of 1974 (FERPA) clarified student and parent's rights regarding school records. This law, introduced in an earlier chapter, is explained in great detail later under the section titled *The Buckley Amendment*.

The legal rights of young children in schools are at best uncertain. This may be particularly true when considering the issue of privacy.

Another area of students' rights, the right to due process, covers a range of issues from discipline to minimum competency testing.

Essentially, the intent of due process, as provided by the Fourteenth Amendment, is to protect students from actions and regulations that are inherently unfair.

Procedural due process
Substantive due process

Parents' Rights

Distinguishing the lines between students' rights, parents' rights, and the school's obligation to educate all children is not an easy task. This is particularly true when reviewing issues involving school counseling services. A parent's right to be involved varies from case to case and from situation to situation.

To date, no federal court rulings have addressed specifically guidance and counseling activities and parents' rights to determine the appropriateness of these services for their children. For now, a critical condition would seem to be whether or not school counseling services are considered essential to the educational program and if written documents verify this relationship in the state and local system.

The Buckley Amendment

This legislation (FERPA) gives parents of minor students (and students eighteen years of age or older) the right to review all official school records related to their children (or themselves in the case of eligible students). FERPA also sets guidelines for disseminating educational records.

Generally, the implementation of FERPA, subsequent interpretations by legislators, and court rulings seem to indicate that the law and its regulations do not necessarily require disclosure of private counseling notes.

Public Law 94-142

In 1975 Congress passed the now famous *Education For All Handicapped Children Act*, commonly called Public Law 94-142. The law guarantees a free and appropriate education to all students regardless of the nature and degree of their handicapping condition.

Even though the role of counselors in this law is not spelled out, school counselors offer many vital services to exceptional students of all categories.

Child Abuse

All states and the District of Columbia have passed legislation addressing child abuse and the obligation of school personnel to report suspected cases. Any provision of privileged communication for students is superseded by a state's desire to protect children from abuse.

Counselor Liability

In serving a wide audience of students, parents, and teachers, school counselors occasionally become concerned about malpractice and professional liability. Malpractice suits typically address two types of liability: civil liability and criminal liability.

While proof of criminal wrongdoing rests with the prosecuting office of the county, state, or federal government, the proof of malpractice in civil liability lies with the plaintiff who brings suit against the counselor.

In general, the following behaviors and services present the most risk for school counselors:
1. <u>Administering drugs</u>.
2. <u>Student searches</u>.
3. <u>Birth control and abortion counseling</u>.
4. <u>Use of student records</u>.

Title IX

The primary purpose of Title IX of the Education Amendments of 1972 is to protect students against discrimination on the basis of sex. If schools violate this law, the penalty is loss of federal financial assistance.

Exercises

1. Research recent court decisions and other legal sources to determine what rulings have been made regarding guidance activities for students in school. Look for decisions that affect students' rights, parents' rights, and the obligation of the school to provide a sound curriculum.
   Rationale: One area that continues to present a legal dilemma for school counselors is affective education through activities such as classroom and small group guidance. Knowledge of current rulings will be helpful.

2. Interview a local attorney who concentrates on educational law and ask about the most important legal issues pertaining to the practice of school counseling. Determine what the local perceptions and norms are about these issues.
Rationale: Local perceptions about legal issues are an essential starting point for all new counselors.

3. Create a fictional situation in which a school counselor could find that ethical standards come in conflict with policies or regulations. Present your situation to the class for discussion.
Rationale: Using case studies or fictional situations helps students practice their responses to ethical and legal dilemmas.

Test Questions

Multiple Choice Items

(b) 1. Ethical standards for the school counseling profession
(a) provide current legal guidelines for professional practice.
(b) offer a general framework for professional practice and responsible behavior.
(c) are absolute guidelines counselors must adhere to.
(d) prohibit private practice.

(c) 2. The term used to indicate that a person is protected from having confidential information revealed in a public hearing or court of law is
(a) common grounds.
(b) *writ of certiorari.*
(c) privileged communication.
(d) a writ of self-disclosure.

(d) 3. Local school board policies are
(a) in contradiction with ethical standards of the counseling profession.
(b) always in agreement with ethical guidelines of counselors.
(c) of little importance to school counselors because they are revised so frequently.
(d) legal guidelines for school personnel to follow.

<u>(a)</u>   4. The intent of due process, as provided by the 14th
                   Amendment to the US Constitution is to protect
                (a) students from actions and regulations that are inherently
                   unfair.
                (b) schools from law suits that have no merit.
                (c) parents from being prosecuted for the misbehaviors of their
                   children.
                (d) students from physical punishment in schools.

<u>(b)</u>   5. The federal law that guides schools in monitoring their
                   collection and use of students' records is the
                (a) National Record Keeping and Paper Reduction Bill of
                   1977.
                (b) Family Educational Rights and Privacy Act of 1974.
                (c) Mental Health Records Act of 1964.
                (d) Title IX of the Educational Amendments of 1972.

<u>(c)</u>   6. In cases of students from divorced parents, both the
                   custodial and non-custodial parent have legal
                   right to see their child's school records unless
                (a) the child waives that right in open court.
                (b) the school has legitimate objection.
                (c) a judge rules otherwise.
                (d) one parent is illiterate.

<u>(a)</u>   7. Students are protected from discrimination on the basis of
                   gender according to
                (a) Title IX of the Educational Amendments of 1972.
                (b) Sex Fair Act of 1956.
                (c) Family Rights and Privacy Act of 1974.
                (d) the Fifteenth Amendment to the US Constitution.

<u>(c)</u>   8. The ethical code for school counselors suggests that
                   counselors are
                (a) beholding to the administrators who hired them.
                (b) absolutely obliged to keep information confidential when
                   counseling students.
                (c) responsible to both their clients and the institutions that
                   employ them.
                (d) prohibited from counseling parents and teachers.

_(c)_ 9. In cases of suspected child abuse,
- (a) school counselors are exempt from reporting laws.
- (b) school principals are the only school officials who may file reports.
- (c) all school personnel are required by law to report.
- (d) parents must be notified by the school if a teacher makes a report.

_(c)_ 10. Students are protected from "unreasonable searches" under the
- (a) child abuse reporting law.
- (b) 1st Amendment to the U.S. Constitution.
- (c) 4th Amendment to the U.S. Constitution.
- (d) Family Rights and Privacy Act of 1974.

Matching Items

COLUMN A		COLUMN B	
_(b)_	ethical standards	A.	circuit courts
_(c)_	case law	B.	guidelines for professional practice
_(a)_	district courts	C.	court rulings
_(e)_	writ of certiorari	D.	Goss v. Lopez
_(d)_	due process	E.	issued by the Supreme Court

Chapter 12

School Counseling Today and Tomorrow

OBJECTIVES

(1) Explore what the future may hold for students of tomorrow.
(2) Present critical issues for students and schools in the future.
(3) Relate these prognostications to the role of school counselors.

CHAPTER SUMMARY

Throughout its development, the school counseling profession has been influenced by educational and social trends, both inside and outside the United States, and has responded to these events by way of federal legislation, state initiatives, and changes within the profession itself.

Today the counseling profession continues to react to social, economic, and political forces of the times, but it also has begun to establish for itself a direction and focus on the future. Futuristic projections for the profession include a wide spectrum of factors including programmatic issues, technological advances, an emerging global economy, and more. This chapter highlights two primary elements because they incorporate all the others: the students and schools of tomorrow.

KEY CONCEPTS

- Redefining families
- Remedial concerns
- Prevention
- Development
- Poverty
- Diversity
- Parental involvement
- School-based services

Students of Tomorrow

As with students today, students in the future will require services to develop skills, acquire information, and attain knowledge to make appropriate decisions about relationships, educational goals, and career aspirations. Most likely, tomorrow's students will not be spared the challenges of human existence and the expected hardship of forging successful careers. For this reason, future school counselors should create expanded visions to meet the needs of a wide range of students.

Remedial Concerns

In addition to the changing family structure, students of tomorrow might exhibit a range of personal, social, physical, and educational concerns emanating from serious ills of society.

School counselors who ignore threatening and debilitating situations, and thereby focus only on students who require information or instruction, will neglect a significant portion of their schools' populations. Future counseling programs must maintain a balance of services to meet the needs of a wide spectrum of students, including those with serious problems.

Preventive Issues

Students in the immediate future will need the same information and education about how to prevent abuse, disease, pregnancy and other life-threatening and debilitating conditions as the students of today require. Schools and counselors who maintain a futuristic vision will constantly seek ways and create methods that enable students to alter their goals, acquire new skills, cope with transitions, and adapt to emerging trends.

Developmental Needs

Students of the next century will have the same biological, emotional, social, and educational expectations as do students of today.

Automation and technology undoubtedly will have an affect on the developmental concerns of students, particularly in regard to career exploration and decision-making. Developmental guidance and counseling activities reflect the belief that students will benefit from lessons and relationships designed to enhance their individual dignity and worth. At the same time, their goal is to teach responsible behaviors.

Two other phenomena will have a tremendous impact on the students' of tomorrow: poverty and diversity.

Poverty

All initiatives at local and national levels to move schools and students to the next century may be wasted unless we pay attention to growing economic disparities in this country and the world. If this trend continues, economic inequality will become a wedge that clearly, more than ever before, divides students of tomorrow into the have's and have nots.

Diversity

Current predictions are that the United States will more closely reflect the cultural and racial balance of the globe by the end of the next century. If these predictions come true and schools eventually reflect this balance, in 21st Century schools cultural diversity will become the norm. The future needs of students from diverse cultural and socioeconomic backgrounds will be addressed by a wide range of counseling and educational services enabling individual students to establish an identity and accept a beneficial role within the school community.

Schools of Tomorrow

We can expect tomorrow's schools to reflect the diversity of U.S. society.

Aspects of nine trends are presented here to illustrate their potential impact on future schools.
1. The population of the United States will slow and mature at the same time.
2. Minority populations, particularly Asians, are expected to expand significantly.
3. Increased demands for services, including education, will put greater strain on already over-stretched state and federal budgets.
4. The ever-changing information technology will have a continuous effect on communications, and on how people work and live.
5. The United States' role as an economic, industrial, and military leader will change as the world moves towards globalization.

6. Medical developments and health care issues, on one hand, will improve the quality of life for many people, and on the other will be criteria that separate people according to their ability to pay for services.

7. Economic, technological, and governmental changes in this and other countries will facilitate a restructuring of business and industry world wide.

8. The family unit will be a stabilizing factor amidst all this change.

9. To a degree, social issues will replace concerns about economic growth and development that dominated most recent decades.

Technology

New and expanded technology will influence every aspect of learning, including guidance activities and counseling services. School counselors will be actively involved in planning and using technology to deliver services to a wide range of students, parents, and teachers.

The future use of technology by counselors depends on how they view the potential value of these tools. Counselors who use a positive language to describe these new services will be able to re-conceptualize their role in schools and integrate advanced technology with helping relationships and learning processes to benefit students.

Parental Involvement

In the future, school counselors will play a significant role in establishing communication and strengthening relationships between parents and schools.

Teacher Collaboration

In addition to working more closely with parents, teachers in the future will collaborate with each other to ensure that all students have an opportunity to receive adequate instruction and achieve accordingly in their academic pursuits. If, as predicted, parental involvement becomes an essential ingredient of future schools, teachers will be front-line collaborators with parents. Of all the trends predicted, this partnership has the most potential for improving schools and education in the 21st Century.

School-Based Services

In past years, school counselors have assumed the role of referral agents, helping students and families locate and receive appropriate services to address an array of challenges. With divergent student populations and the likelihood that additional and expanded services for these students and their families will be needed, school-based service models may provide an efficient and effective alternative to outside referrals.

Youth Service

Another trend in U.S. schools involves programs that combine classroom instruction with social service and activism. Known collectively as youth service programs, many of these are already implemented in schools across the country and cover a range of projects from performing environmental clean-up to operating day-care programs.

The Future of School Counseling

As students and schools enter the 21st Century and confront the range of changes and challenges predicted for the future, school counselors must be ready to assist. To meet these challenges, future counselors will:
1. Develop a broader knowledge of human development throughout the life span.
2. Adapt to new technology.
3. Increase the use of group processes.
4. Expand their professional development.
5. Measure the outcome of their services.

Exercises

1. Go to a school and ask a small group of students to design a school of the future. In helping with their designs you might suggest that they consider: What school buildings of the future might be like, what will classroom have that are not there today, and what will students be like?
   Rationale: As part of creating their own vision of the future, counselor education students might benefit from hearing the perspectives of students in elementary and secondary schools.

2. In this chapter we have predicted some possibilities for school counseling in the future. What does your future hold? Brainstorm by yourself and list ten things that will be different about your life in the future. Share this list with a classmate. How many things on both of your lists will you have control over? How many things

will be inevitable? What will these changes mean for you as a professional counselor?

Rationale: A competent counselor consistently evaluates his or her perceptions and adjusts those perceptions to meet future goals.

Test Questions

Multiple Choice Items

(a) 1. Future projections suggest that American society will
 (a) continue to become more diverse.
 (b) regress to a more homogeneous culture.
 (c) be drug free.
 (d) be guided by extreme affluence in most all segments of the population.

(b) 2. One factor that will be a major influence on schools of the future will be the
 (a) political elections at the local school level.
 (b) success or failure of the U.S. to address the problem of poverty.
 (c) return to community schools.
 (d) student outcomes from end of course testing.

(c) 3. In the future, school counselors may be expected to
 (a) hold dual certification as administrations.
 (b) teach psychology classes.
 (c) work with younger populations, i.e., preschoolers.
 (d) acquire doctoral degrees.

(c) 4. Presently, the rapidly advancing computer technology
 (a) is having tremendous impact on the delivery of counseling services in schools.
 (b) has stagnated counseling programs.
 (c) has had little noticeable impact on counseling services for students.
 (d) is not likely to be important in school counseling.

(b) 5. Parental involvement in schools
 (a) is not an area of concern for counselors.
 (b) has been related to higher student achievement.
 (c) should be discouraged if professionals are to maintain control of our schools.
 (d) is not as important in upper grades as it is in elementary schools.

<u>(b)</u>   6. The school counseling profession
          (a) is in serious trouble due to the loss of thousands of
              positions across the country.
          (b) has one of the highest memberships among the divisions of
              the American Counseling Association.
          (c) is less able and proficient than other counseling specialties.
          (d) will no longer be important as other helping specialties
              enter schools in larger numbers.

<u>(b)</u>   7. If the prediction of having more school-based services
             comes true,
          (a) fewer school counselors will be needed.
          (b) school counselors will be assisted by in-school medical,
              psychological, and social services staff members.
          (c) the role of the teacher will be diminished.
          (d) parents will no longer need to search for services outside
              the school.

<u>(c)</u>   8. In the future, we can expect that school counselors will
          (a) not need to be concerned about remedial issues.
          (b) require less training in human development.
          (c) continue to provide a balance of remedial, preventive,
              and developmental services.
          (d) be replaced by technological advances.

<u>(b)</u>   9. Professionally, school counselors
          (a) are not as well-trained as mental health counselors.
          (b) comprise one of the largest divisions of the American
              Counseling Association.
          (c) can expect to be replaced by "guidance technicians" in
              the future.
          (d) will need doctoral training to be successful in the future.

<u>(d)</u>   10. The following trend is expected in future school
             counseling programs.
          (a) Less use of technology.
          (b) Less direct counseling services.
          (c) More work with students in crisis.
          (d) More group work with students, parents, and teachers.